The Great Debate

THE
GREAT DEBATE

CALVINISM, ARMINIANISM AND SALVATION

ALAN P. F. SELL

WIPF & STOCK PUBLISHERS
790 East 11th ◆ Eugene OR 97401

1998

The Great Debate
Calvinism, Arminianism and Salvation

By Sell, Alan P.F.
Copyright©1998 Sell, Alan P.F.

ISBN: 1-57910-113-5

Printed by WIPF & STOCK PUBLISHERS *1998*
790 East 11th ♦ Eugene OR 97401

Previously Published by H. E. Walter Ltd., 1982

Contents

Preface

'In the work of salvation, does God need man's help?' 'Is man totally, or only partially, powerless to help himself?' These are two rather crude ways of putting questions which are central to the Christian family dispute between Calvinists and Arminians. For nearly four hundred years many changes were rung upon these themes, until the main debate ended inconclusively with a whimper during the later years of the nineteenth century.

Scattered and sometimes partisan references to this theological debate may be found in the denominational, and other, histories. My aim is to tell an intriguing and complex story in a continuous, balanced way, and within reasonable compass. I trust that the notes will assist those who wish to pursue matters further, and that the glossary will assist the general reader and not distress the expert.

I fully recognise that the ramifications of my theme are manifold. It would have been possible, for example, to have asked, 'How far were seventeenth-century Calvinists influenced in their theological methodology by rationalism — even by that of the rationalistic Arminians, in so far as they sought to play them at their own game?'. But this would have taken us too far afield; and as for the rationalistic Arminians, I have paid some attention to them in an article entitled, 'Arminians, Deists and Reason', in *Faith and Freedom,* Autumn 1979. I here seek to follow my selected doctrinal thread closely in the quest of clarity, and at the risk of a measure of abstraction. Indeed I feel that the advantages of treating my chosen cluster of issues in some detail more than outweigh the disadvantages which attend the discussion of any single doctrine in isolation. Not least among these advantages is that as we follow our authors in their efforts to understand the respective parts played by God and man in the matter of man's salvation, we shall be brought face to face with the question, 'What is the heart of the Christian gospel?'. The Calvinists and Arminians themselves were well aware of this, and they prompt me to ask two questions: 'Even if we feel disinclined to re-open the debate in their terms, are we satisfied that the question of the heart of the gospel is in our time engaging enough theologians in lively, charitable, ecumenical debate?' And, 'Now that the dust of controversy has largely settled, do the old Calvinist-Arminian disputes afford any clues as to the points upon which we need to be clear if our proclamatory trumpets are not to make an uncertain sound?'. My interests are thus by no means exclusively antiquarian. I offer my chronicle, and I ask my questions.

Dr. G. F. Nuttall has, as so often, been generous in encouragement, and searching in criticism. For this I am deeply grateful. I need hardly add that I lay exclusive claim to any surviving perversities.

Alan P. F. Sell
West Midlands College of Higher Education,
Walsall.

CHAPTER ONE

The Source

The celebrated Scottish divine, Dr. John 'Rabbi' Duncan, thought that unlike Calvinism, both Arminianism and antinomianism made false starts: 'Antinomianism says that we (to use the words of Towne) are Christ-ed and God-ed. Arminianism says that half the work is God's and half is man's. Calvinism asserts that the whole is God's and the whole is man's also.'[1] We here attempt to trace the course of the four-hundred-year-long debate upon the issues thus somewhat baldly encapsulated.

In the quest of clarity we must first discuss some terminological questions. Thus, for example, even when Calvin has enjoyed the favour of true representation, it has not always been remembered that the Calvin*ism* against which Arminius (1560—1609) protested was the high supralapsarianism of Calvin's disciple Theodore Beza (1519—1605). Again, the cluster of doctrines often branded 'Arminian' owe as much to his followers as 'they do to Arminius himself. Certainly Arminius denied the teaching of his disciple Philipp von Limborch (1633—1712) to the effect that there was heaven for believers, hell for those who had refused Christ, and an intermediate state for those who had had no opportunity of hearing the gospel. And, as we shall see, Arminius had not reached a firm conclusion on the question of the perseverance of the saints when he died. Finally, developing Arminianism flowed into two theoretically and temperamentally dissimilar, and sometimes opposed, streams. Let us further elucidate these points.

That formative thinkers provoke both adulation and hostility is an easily justifiable generalisation. Undeniably Calvin has received sufficient of both. Thus, with reference to the view of some of the eighteenth century Episcopalian clergy, Dr. Cunningham said that 'when they speak of [Calvin] in connection with his view about the divine sovereignty and decrees, we might be tempted to think, from the spirit they often manifest, that they looked upon him almost as if he himself were the author or cause of the fate of those who finally perish'.[2] Making a broader sweep, A. M. Fairbairn averred:

> 'There is something imposing in the multitude and variety of aversions that converge on Calvin. He was hated by Catholics as the author of the system that opposed the proudest and most invincible front to Rome; by princes and statesmen, as the man who instituted a Church that acted as a revolutionary force in politics; by Anglican bishops and divines, as the father of the Puritanism that so long disturbed their power; by Arminian theologians as the inventor and apologist of a *decretum horribile* which they detested, without always making sure that they understood; by Free thinkers, as the man that burned Servetus . . . But the man who has touched so many men, discordant in everything but this concordance of hate, must have been a man of transcendent power . . .'[3]

In our opinion it is perverse to suggest, as some have done, that Calvin was a narrow-minded dogmatist, who so exalted his favourite doctrine, predestination, as to expel all real religion from Christianity, and to land us in a remorselessly logical cerebralism from which Augustine's ecclesiastical palliatives were expunged.

In the first place, Calvin was not narrow-minded. This means three things: (a) his writings display an extensive and practical concern for the right ordering of life under God, and are not exclusively concerned with the allegedly morbid aspects of theology;[4] (b) despite his physical frailty and frequent pain, Calvin was quite able to enjoy himself — as John Knox discovered when he found Calvin playing bowls on the Lord's day;[5] (c) Calvin's humanist training, though modified after his evangelical conversion in 1533, remained influential throughout his life. He was ever in touch with, and broadly appreciative of, the best in the culture of his day, and his passion for education owed more than a little to the impetus of humanism.[6] Indeed, we may say that Calvin's Platonist-humanist background made him more flexible in his thinking than the Aristotelian rationalism of some of the more scholastic Calvinists who followed him. Philip C. Holtrop has put the point well: 'In Calvin the concepts of predestination and foreknowledge have little to do with deterministic schema and much to do with the sureness and purposiveness and rootedness of God's history of salvation and present saving activity *in Christo;* that is to say, eternity and history have everything to do with each other'.[7]

Secondly, the charge that Calvin's primary doctrine is predestination, and that he delighted to unravel the intricacies of its fearful logic is wide of the mark. Predestination is a central doctrine in Calvin's system, but it is not primary. It is a derivative of his doctrine of God's sovereignty and, more-over, it does not receive its exposition in the *Institutes* in connection with God's nature; it appears much later, towards the end of Book III, in connection with the way in which men receive the grace of Christ. The question whether Calvin makes the quasi-pantheistic will of God paramount (and this is what is feared or assumed by those who make the point we are querying) rather than God's electing grace, is one to which we shall have to return.[8] Our preliminary judgment is that Beza was more guilty in this direction than Calvin, for 'By developing a supralapsarian scheme . . . [he] lifted the doctrine of predestination to a position of priority far above that given to it by Calvin'.[9] If we *had* to find a slogan definition of Calvin we should concur with Dr. John Hesselink in denominating him 'The theologian of the Holy Spirit', in recognition of his reliance upon God the Holy Spirit in his view of *renewed* man's ability; of God's providential order; of the authority of scripture; of the Christian life; and of the Church and the sacraments. In Calvin's thought the key to all of these is God the Holy Spirit.[10]

Thirdly, as to the bogeyman of logical rigour, the slightest acquaintance with the works of Calvin suffices to assure one that confronted by irresolvable antinomies, Calvin never declines an *O altitudo!* This is true, not least in connection with the *decretum horribile* of predestination to damnation, where the positive intention is the maintenance of the notion of God's justice in judging sin. Again, Calvin's view that whilst the gospel is to be proclaimed to all, it is not in the strictest sense *for* any but the elect, is one which he is content to leave in the logically awkward state in which he found it. Finally, as to the alleged iciness which is supposed by some to accompany logical rigour, it should not be forgotten that Calvin was the subject of an evangelical conversion experience — he was not unacquainted with, or unfavourably disposed towards, the religion of the heart. True, Calvin's conversion experience is not as well known as Luther's, Bunyan's or Wesley's — not to mention Paul's; for one thing, Calvin himself said comparatively little about it. As Dr. J. T. McNeill reminds us, it was not until long after the event that he wrote 'God by a sudden conversion subdued my heart to teachableness'; and Dr. McNeill asks, 'In this familiar sentence, have we duly felt the force of his word "teachableness"? Heart and intellect were alike quickened and redirected'.[11] We are back, once more, to God the Holy Spirit; and we have here a man who was something more than a cold splitter of theological hairs![12]

We may perhaps allow our Victorian mentors to encapsulate for us the positive *intentions* of Calvinism:

'Calvinism is just a full exposition and development of the sum and substance of what is represented in Scripture as done for the salvation of sinners by the three persons of the Godhead. It represents the Father as arranging, in accordance with all the perfections of His nature and all the principles of His moral government, and at the same time, with due regard to the actual capacities and obligations of men, the whole provisions of the scheme of redemption, choosing some men to grace and glory, and sending His Son to seek and save them. It represents the Son as assuming human nature, and suffering and dying as the Surety and Substitute of His chosen people . . . as doing and bearing everything necessary for securing their eternal salvation. It represents the Holy Spirit as taking of the things of Christ and showing them to men's souls, as . . . applying the blessings of redemption to all for whom Christ purchased them, and finally preparing them fully for the inheritance of the saints.'[13]

Fairbairn is more concise: 'The strength of Calvinism lay in the place and pre-eminence it gave to God: it magnified Him; humbled man before His awful majesty, yet lifted man in the very degree that it humbled him'.[14]

We shall shortly summarise those of Calvin's doctrines which were central to the Calvinist-Arminian dispute, but we must first provide a brief statement of the context within which Arminius himself worked; for in this respect, as in regard to the actual things he taught, Arminius has been almost as grievously misunderstood as has Calvin. We must first make plain that Arminianism arose as a genuine option *within,* and not as a parasite upon, the Reformed Church in Holland. Professor Carl Bangs, a leading authority on Arminianism, has shown that

> 'there was one broad stream of Dutch Reformed life and thought which was declared out of bounds by Dort. At the time it was called Remonstrantism or Arminianism, but it antedated both the Remonstrance of 1610 and Arminius . . . The fact that this more diffuse source of the Dutch Reformation could embrace the humanist or "Libertine" Dirk Volckertz Coornhert, who belonged to no church, should not shut our eyes to the inclusion also of Johannes à Lasco, Johannes Utenhove, and Martinus Micronius, who can scarcely be described as Calvinists. Nor should the movement be described as a "third force", something not genuinely related to what emerged as the Dutch Reformed Church. There was an intermingling of the "Dutch National Reformation" and more strictly Calvinist-Reformed currents, and they did not get segregated until Dort.'[15]

As for Arminius himself, he did not set out to be a 'troubler of Israel'. He never forsook his belief in predestination (though he opposed Beza's formulation of the doctrine); he was not, and refused to be labelled, a Pelagian; and to the end he professed loyalty to the Confessions of his Church: 'I confidently declare that I have never taught anything . . . which contravenes the sacred writings that ought to be with us the sole rule of thinking and of speaking, or which is opposed to the Belgic Confession or to the Heidelberg Catechism.'[16] What he positively affirmed we shall shortly see.

Our final piece of preliminary ground-clearing has to do with the increasing ambiguity of 'Arminianism' as the term came to be employed. Leaving on one side its use as a nickname (Cf. the early usage of 'Quaker', Methodist' etc.), there developed two main varieties of Arminianism. There is what Dr. Nuttall has described as an 'Arminianism of the head', and an 'Arminianism of the heart'.[17] The former emphasises man's liberty, and this expresses itself in a concern for freedom of thought and freedom of life — that is, toleration (with the proviso that England offers a rather special case; for with the notable exception of such dissenters as John Goodwin and John Smyth, it suited the Laudian party of Anglican Arminians to *oppose* toleration, whilst at the same time paving the way for Latitudinarian theology). Into the rationalising tendencies of this form of Arminianism we shall not here enquire, but shall rather adhere closely to the trail of the doctrinal dispute concerning the God-man relation. The latter variety of Arminianism is of the evangelical kind. It has very much to do with man's ability to respond to God's grace — a grace freely available to all who will claim it. In this connection we shall meet the Wesleys, and over against them, Whitefield; and, from the ranks of the Baptists, Andrew Fuller, whose evangelically inspired attitudes placed him in opposition to the High Calvinists of his own denomination and beyond, and did so much to inspire the modern missionary movement.

To borrow an ugly phrase from the world of trade unionism, we are here concerned with a 'Who does what?' dispute. The question is, 'In the matter of man's salvation, who is doing the saving — God? or man? or God and man together?'. Those hostile to Arminianism have seen it as a step on the road to Pelagianism, though the evangelical Arminians (not to mention Arminius himself) have always resisted this charge. They have presented their view as one which both honours God's justice (whereas, they contend, Calvinism exalts his caprice), and upholds man's proper dignity as a child of God (as against what they take to be Calvinism's reduction of man to an automaton). With these somewhat sweeping statements we may leave preliminaries, and investigate what Arminius actually taught. Having done this we shall state Calvin's position, and that of his followers, in respect of the points in dispute at Dort; and finally we shall trace the main ripples of the debate in Britain with sidelong glances, as necessary, at the continent and at America.

Arminius's immediate debt was to some of the more liberal of the Renaissance humanists, and his ideas were sharpened against that somewhat rigid variety of Calvinism which reached his native Holland through his own mentor, Beza, and through the latter's colleagues, Petrus Plancius and Franciscus Gomarus (1563–1641). In addition to Erasmus, on the humanist side, there was the Italian Bernardino Ochino (1487–1564), whose pilgrimage within the Roman Church led him from the Observatine Franciscans to the more stringent Capuchins, before his departure for Lutheranism in 1541, under the influence of Peter Martyr (1500–62). Whilst on a visit to England Ochino wrote his *The Labyrinth* against Calvin's pre-destinarianism. Other humanists such as Uytenbogaert, Corvinus and Vondel advanced criticisms of Calvinism, but, above all, there was Dirk Volkertz Coornhert (1522–90). He advocated toleration, opposed the capital punishment of heretics, denied the need of the visible Church, and veered in the direction of pietism. Calvin's *Résponse à un certain Hollandais* (1562) was a criticism of his position. Nor was England free from humanist, liberalising influence. For example, the Frenchman Peter Baro (1534–99), during his period as Professor at Cambridge (1574–96) opposed the pre-destinarian teaching of his colleague William Perkins (1558–1602), and advocated a universalist position.

In opposition to this liberal mood stood Plancius and Beza. Beza emphasised Adam's federal headship of the human race, holding that it entailed universal guilt and pollution. More importantly, he advocated a supralapsarian version of the doctrine of the decrees of God. Thus, for him, the Fall itself was decreed, and along with it the destruction of human freedom; and the whole was alleged to be the means to the outworking of God's pre-mundane determinations regarding the destiny of those whom he *would* create. Of this doctrine James Orr, himself by no means unfavourably disposed towards Calvinism, wrote, 'A doctrine of this kind, which bids us think of beings not yet conceived of as even created (therefore only *possibles*) — not to say as sinful — set apart for eternal blessedness or misery, and of the fall and redemption as simply means for effecting that purpose, is one which no plea of logical consistency will ever get the human mind to accept, and which is bound to provoke revolt against the whole system with which it is associated'.[18]

This was certainly the reaction of Arminius, when he came across Perkin's *De Praedestinationis Modo et Ordine* — a restatement of Beza's views — in 1598. In the same year Arminius wrote a reply, though it was not published until after his death. Ten years earlier, in 1588, Arminius, who had just become a minister in Amsterdam, incurred the wrath of his senior colleague, Plancius, because in expounding *Romans* 7:14 ff he argued that Paul's meaning was that the unregenerate, not the regenerate, experienced the agony of the gulf between the demands of the law and their inability to meet those demands. What finally brought matters to a head was Arminius's relationship with the supralapsarian Gomarus (who had been Professor at Leyden since 1594, and whose colleague there Arminius became in 1603, on the death, by plague, of Franciscus Junius), and his conscientious inability to accept the invitation of some fellow churchmen to *defend* supralapsarianism *against* Dirk Volkertz Coornhert.

It became increasingly incumbent upon Arminius to make his position clear and public, and this he did in his *Declaration* to the Lords of the States of Holland on 30th October 1608.[19] In his preamble Arminius reminded his hearers that Gomarus had taken so serious a view of his colleague's opinions as to say that he would not dare to appear before his Maker with such views, and that Arminian teaching would, unless stopped, cause civil war.[20] There follows a lengthy description of the abortive attempts thus far to bring Arminius before what he deemed to be unequal and unconstitutional assemblies. He then comes to doctrine, and first outlines the generally received supralapsarian teaching which it is his purpose to refute. He points out that the Calvinists regard any contradiction of their view as tantamount to denying glory to God, and to ascribing salvation to man — as being, in a word, Pelagianism.[21] His contrary contention is that supralapsarian predestination is not the foundation of Christianity, of salvation, or of assurance. The decree fundamental to Christianity is God's appointment of Christ to be Saviour, and in this (and not in God's inscrutable will) our salvation rests. Moreover, the believer's assurance depends upon the decree, ' "They who believe, shall be saved": I believe, therefore I shall be saved. But the doctrine of this Predestination embraces within itself neither the first nor the second member of the syllogism'.[22] Indeed, it positively excludes the gospel, for the gospel consists 'partly of an injunction *to repent and believe,* and partly of a promise to bestow *forgiveness of sins, the Spirit of grace, and life eternal*', but the supralapsarian position cannot accommodate such matters.[23]

Arminius proceeds to argue that supralapsarianism can be found neither in the credal deliverances of the ancient Church, nor in the confessional statements of the Reformed and Protestant Churches. The doctrine is, in detail, offensive for many reasons. It is a libel against God's nature, and in particular against his wisdom, justice and goodness; for it presents him as creating something 'for eternal perdition to the praise of his justice'[24] thereby, allegedly, demonstrating his mercy and justice by a decree which is contrary to both. Further, God's goodness is flouted by making him will 'the greatest evil to his creatures'.[25] Again, supralapsarianism abuses man, for it denies that man was created in God's image, with that freedom of will whereby he is able freely to know God and holiness. The doctrine of creation is undermined, because *God* creates what is good, not what is reprobate; God's glory is injured, for supralapsarianism makes him the author of sin; Jesus, not being involved in the decree of predestination, is no longer the foundation or the meritorious cause of election; and the believer's proper godly sorrow for sin, and his zeal and holiness and prayer, are redundant. Supralapsarianism inverts the order of the gospel which is that salvation is consequent upon repentance and faith, for it decides the issue of a man's end in eternity. Christian ministers are thereby encouraged to be slothful and negligent — for, on the supralapsarian view, if the doctrine which ministers preach is sound, it can benefit nobody; if it is unsound, it can harm nobody: all is predetermined. In fact, supralapsarianism *'completely subverts* the foundation of religion in general, *and of the Christian Religion in particular*'.[26] It inverts the order and mutual relations of God's two-fold love, whereby he loves righteousness (and hates sin), and loves man (and therefore rewards those who seek him with eternal life). Supralapsarianism admits the possibility that God will save some whether they seek him or not, and that he will damn others without regard to their actual disobedience. Finally, *'this doctrine of Predestination* has been rejected *both in former times and in our own days,* by the greater part of the professors of Christianity'[27] — not least by (the later) Luther and Melanchthon, and by the Dane Nicholas Hemmingus (1513– 1600).

Arminius next briefly reviews modified supralapsarianism and infralapsarianism. He grants that they both seek to avoid making God the author of sin; and that both deny that the fall is the mediate, foreordained and necessary cause of the execution of the decree of predestination. This apart, he contends that the arguments adduced against strict supralapsarianism hold also against its modifications. He then sets down his positive understanding of predestination in four points:-

1. The *first* absolute decree of God concerning the salvation of sinful man, is that by which he decreed to appoint his Son Jesus Christ for a Mediator, Redeemer, Saviour, Priest and King, who might destroy sin by his own death, might by his obedience obtain the salvation which had been lost, and might communicate it by his own virtue.

2. The *second* precise and absolute decree of God, is that in which he decreed to receive into his favour *those who repent and believe,* and, in Christ, for His sake and through Him, to effect the salvation of such penitents and believers as persevered to the end; but to leave in sin and under wrath *all impenitent persons and unbelievers,* and to damn them as aliens from Christ.

3. The *third* Divine decree is that by which God decreed to administer *in a sufficient and efficacious manner* the means which were necessary for repentance and faith; and to have such administration instituted (1) according to the *Divine Wisdom,* by which God knows what is proper and becoming both to his mercy and his severity, and (2) accord-

ing to *Divine Justice,* by which He is prepared to adopt whatever his wisdom may prescribe and to put it in execution.

4. To these succeeds the *fourth* decree, by which God decreed to save and damn certain particular persons. This decree has its foundation in the foreknowledge of God, by which he knew from all eternity those individuals who *would,* through his preventing grace, *believe,* and, through his subsequent grace *would persevere,* — according to the before-described administration of those means which are suitable and proper for conversion and faith; and, by which foreknowledge, he likewise knew those who *would not believe and persevere.'*[28]

Arminius contends that the position thus defined accords well with all truly Christian teaching on God, man, sin and salvation; it honours God's grace and makes Christ central to the redemptive process; it does not undermine the ministry of the Church, nor make earnest Christian practice pointless; in short, it is in harmony with ancient and modern orthodox belief.

There follow some brief statements on cognate doctrines. Man's will is said to be in subjection to God's providence; but whereas God wills and performs good acts, he merely freely permits evil acts. Before the fall man could, with the assistance of divine grace, perform truly good acts; but fallen man requires 'to be regenerated and renewed in intellect, affections or will, and in all his powers, by God in Christ through the Holy Spirit, that he may be qualified rightly to understand, esteem, consider, will, and perform whatever is truly good. When he is made a partaker of this regeneration or renovation, I consider that, since he is delivered from sin, he is capable of thinking, willing, and doing that which is good, but yet *not without the continued aids of Divine Grace'.*[29] (It is not easy to read pure Pelagianism into this!)

For Arminius, divine grace is a gratuitous affection, an infusion of the gifts of the Holy Spirit, and a perpetual assistance to the renewed man. As to the perseverance of the saints: those who have been grafted into Christ possess sufficient powers to fight Satan with the Spirit's aid — though Synod ought diligently to enquire 'Whether it is not possible for some individuals through negligence to desert the commencement of their existence in Christ . . . and to cause Divine grace to be ineffectual'.[30] Arminius has never actually taught the final falling away of the true believer, and he does uphold the believer's right to assurance. As to whether a believer can perfectly obey God in this life (with the Spirit's aid, and not in a Pelagian sense), this is, he thinks, an open question; though, with the support of Augustine, he does not deny the possibility. As to the divinity of the Son of God, Arminius defines αὐτοθεος in two senses: (a) 'one who is truly God', and (b) 'one who is God of himself'. He accepts the former, but not the latter. On the question of justification, Arminius finds himself at one with all the Reformed and Protestant Churches. With a lengthy plea that the Dutch Confession and Catechism should be examined at a properly convened Synod, and with an expression of his hope that doctrinal disagreement will not lead to ecclesiastical schism, Arminius concludes his *Declaration*.

Although Arminius had no difficulty with the Heidelberg Catechism, his interpretation of Article XVI of the Belgic Confession, in its pre-Dort version, caused some consternation. The article declared that God is 'merciful in that he delivers and saves out of this ruination those whom he in his eternal and unchangeable council [*sic*], through his pure goodness has elected and chosen in Jesus Christ our Lord, without any consideration of their good works . . .'[31] As Professor Bangs points out, Arminius (against the Calvinistic stream) understood this to mean that those chosen in Christ are believers, and not that God predetermines who will be believers.[32] This was a legitimate and legally correct interpretation before the Synod of Dort, but in other respects the debate between Arminius and his opponents was finely balanced. So much so that Bangs can show with some relish that both Gomarus and Arminius unwittingly gave their respective cases away. Arminius held to the election of believers, and Gomarus conceded this point in his thirty-second thesis. For his part, Arminius 'threw over his whole case in adding a predestination of individuals on the basis of a necessary foreknowledge of future things *that shall be*'.[33] (It is important to notice in passing that unlike some who subsequently took his name, Arminius was not an unconditional universalist. On the contrary, he maintained that 'God has by a preremptory decree resolved, that believers alone should be partakers of this redemption'.)[34]

The subsequent debate left any mutual inconsistencies unremarked, and concentrated upon the question of man's responsibility and God's justice. Arminius summed up his view in a letter to Junius: 'God can indeed do what He wills with His own; but He cannot will to do with His own what He cannot rightfully do, for His will is circumscribed within the bounds of justice.' As Fairbairn saw, 'the moment the idea of equity was admitted to a place in the relations of God to man, the old absolute unconditionalism became untenable'.[35] As for man, sin has not entirely removed his ability or his reason; a man inherits evil but not guilt. Thus 'the free will of man came to condition the absolute will of God'.[36] These were the issues which were thrown into relief after the death of Arminius in 1609, when Episcopius (i.e. Simon Bischop, 1583–1643) who, by an irony of history, was to succeed Gomarus at Leyden, assumed the leadership of the Arminian party. We shall not follow all the steps in the ensuing controversy, but shall simply note the points made by the Remonstrants to the civil authorities of the United Provinces in 1610, and the response which these elicited from the Calvinists at the Synod of Dort, 1618–9.

In 1610 the Arminians proposed the following five points: (1) God's decree of election and his decree of reprobation are conditional upon foreknown faith, or lack of it. (2) Christ 'died for all men and for every man, so that he merited reconciliation and forgiveness of sins for all . . . yet so that no one actually enjoys the forgiveness of sins except the believer'. (3) Regeneration by the Holy Spirit is necessary to salvation. (4) Grace is resistible. (5) The final perseverance of believers can neither be denied, nor positively asserted. In the course of time the second point was given a universalistic interpretation by some; the third point, when associated with a less than radical view of total depravity, lost much of its force; and the fifth point was decided by many against the

final perseverance of the saints — a position which some had
reached by the time the Synod of Dort met.

The five Canons of Dort are the obverse of the five Arminian
points, and justice requires us to note that their nature as
responses should caution us against thinking that they represent the *sum* of Calvinism, though they are, of course,
central to it and distinctive of it.[37] The Calvinists asserted
(1) That the decrees of election and reprobation are absolute
and unconditional. (2) That although Christ's death is sufficient to expiate the sins of the whole world, the atonement
is in fact limited to the elect, who are thus certain to be
saved. (3) That the total inability of man to will the good
necessitates the regenerating work of the Holy Spirit. (4) That
God's call is effectual, and hence his grace is irresistible.
(5) That those who are elected and called cannot but be saved,
and cannot finally be lost. It should be observed that,
especially with regard to the second point, we do not here
have the ultra-Calvinism of the Gomarists: there is a decided
softening of doctrine in the interests of ethical considerations.

It remains to reflect upon the points just baldly stated. This
we shall do under the headings of man's plight, man's will[38]
and God's grace. Orthodox Calvinists have ever taken a serious
view of man and his sin. To them, as to Calvin himself, the
essence of sin is not so much pride, as with Augustine and
Aquinas, but unbelief. In this they are at one with Luther.
Fallen man's knowledge of God is vitiated; his life is rendered
abnormal. Man is totally (i.e. in every part) depraved. Yet
fallen man knows enough to know that he *ought* to be at one
with God. He is aware of the law of God — indeed, it is his
greatest threat; it is also his greatest spur to Christ, for
despairing of his inability to fulfil the requirements of the
law, he turns to Christ for grace. Fallen man's ethical estrangement from God is complete. Only when the regenerating
Spirit of God possesses him can be truly see with what kind
of God he has to do; and only then can he begin to lead a
righteous, God-honouring life:

> 'We shall not say that, properly speaking, God is known
> where there is no religion or piety . . . In this ruin of man-
> kind no one now experiences God either as Father or as
> Author of salvation, or favourable in any way, until Christ

the Mediator comes forward to reconcile him to us . . . There is within the human mind, and indeed by natural instinct, an awareness of divinity . . . There are innumerable evidences both in heaven and on earth that declare his wonderful wisdom . . . man . . . is a rare example of God's power . . . But although the Lord represents both himself and his everlasting Kingdom in the mirror of his works with very great clarity, such is our stupidity that we grow increasingly dull towards so manifest testimonies and they flow away without profiting us.'[39]

Man is, however, quite without excuse:

'We are so vitiated and perverted in every part of our nature that by this great corruption we stand justly condemned and convicted before God, to whom nothing is acceptable but righteousness, innocence and purity . . . Not only has punishment fallen upon us from Adam, but a contagion imparted by him resides within us, which justly deserves punishment . . . even infants themselves, while they carry their condemnation along with them from their mother's womb, are guilty not of another's fault but of their own.'[40]

(On this last point Zwingli was out of accord with both Luther and Calvin). However, although God's decretive will must include the sins of men, this is not to be understood as making God the author of sin. Thus, against Pighius (c. 1490– 1542) Calvin urged that

'God in ordaining the fall of man had an end most just and right which holds the name of sin in abhorrence. Though I affirm that He ordained it so, I do not allow that He is properly the author of sin. Not to spend longer on the point, I am of opinion that what Augustine teaches was fulfilled: In a wonderful and ineffable way, what was done contrary to His will was yet not done without His will, because it would not have been done at all unless He had allowed it. So He permitted it not unwillingly but willingly . . . To this opinion of this holy man I subscribe: in sinning they did what God did not will in order that God through their evil might do what He willed. If anyone object that this is beyond comprehension, I confess it. But what

wonder if the immense and incomprehensible majesty of
God exceed the limits of our intellect?'[41]

Thus God is in no way held to ransom by the wicked. He can
accomplish his will through them, whilst 'they are not
excusable, as if they had obeyed his precept which out of
their own lust they deliberately break'.[42]

Arminius, as we have seen, was equally concerned to emphasise that God was not the author of sin. Even William
Cunningham can say that 'the statements of Arminius himself,
in regard to the natural depravity of man, so far as we have
them upon record, are full and satisfactory'.[43] Further, the
Remonstrant points did not mention, and certainly did not
deny, the doctrine of total depravity. There was, however, a
gradual drift from this doctrine on the part of many Arminians,
especially when they came to deny (in opposition to Beza)
the imputation of Adam's first sin to his descendants, and
when they elaborated their view of man's freedom in such a
way as to threaten the notion of man's total inability. Here
we approach the crux of the Calvinist-Arminian dispute.
Cunningham speaks for all his party in recognising a slippery
slope when he sees one: 'when Calvinistic principles are
rejected or thrown into the background, not only is something,
more or less, of necessity taken from the Creator and assigned
to the creature, but an opening is made, – an opportunity is
left, – for carrying on this process of transferring to man what
belongs to God to almost any extent, until the scriptural
method of salvation is wholly set aside or overturned.'[44]

For Calvin, as for Luther, man's will is enslaved. This claim
he defended against those humanists and *quasi*-Arminians (not
to be anachronistic), whether Catholic or Protestant, who
would unduly have exalted fallen man's ability to perform
good works, thereby undermining the absolute need of God's
grace. Calvin urged that 'Because of the bondage of sin by
which the will is held bound, it cannot move towards good,
much less apply itself thereto; for a movement of this sort is
the beginning of conversion to God'.[45] Fallen man's will is
by no means obliterated: 'the will remains, with the most
eager inclination disposed and hastening to sin. For man, when
he gave himself over to this necessity, was not deprived of
will, but of soundness of will.'[46] Hence Calvin's view, in line

with that of Augustine and Luther, that the deeds of fallen man, proceeding as they do from an evil will, are themselves evil: 'I admit that the endowments resplendent in Camillus were gifts of God and seem rightly commendable if judged in themselves . . . [But] as you will not commend a man for virtue when his vices impress you under the appearance of virtues, so you will not attribute to the human will the capability of seeking after the right so long as the will remains set in its own perversity.'[47]

In what sense, then, is man free? Pighius argued in his *De Libero Hominis Arbitrio* (1542) that apart from free-will man could not be responsible; and if he were not responsible, he could not be culpable. Calvin wishes to argue that man's will *is* bound, but that he is still responsible. His freedom consists in his being able to act freely (i.e. not under compulsion or constraint applied from without) in a manner consistent with his will; but fallen man's will is depraved, and from this depravity he can be rescued only by the grace of God in Christ. Then and then only is he truly free — free in principle from sin, and free for the proper service of God. Because 'free-will' is so often construed as 'indeterminancy' Calvin would like to dispense with the word altogether. 'How few men are there, I ask, who when they hear free will attributed to man do not immediately conceive him to be the master of both his own mind and will, able of his own power to turn himself toward either good or evil?'[48] As Dr. Townley Lord has it, Calvin 'was concerned more with *right* will than with *free* will. Right will is the result of divine restoration: thus restored, it chooses the good'.[49] Calvin himself indignantly asks, 'Who shall say that the infirmity of the human will is strengthened by his help in order that it may aspire effectively to the choice of good, when it must rather be wholly transformed and renewed? . . . Not a whit remains to man to glory in, for the whole of salvation comes from God'.[50] This, once more, is the threatened position.

To the Arminians, however, the Calvinists were undermining man's proper dignity: they were making man a puppet. But Calvin denied that he was a necessitarian, and Cunningham has argued in detail that whereas adherents to the Reformed confessions have espoused both necessitarianism and

libertarianism, and notwithstanding the fact that most Reformed thinkers have favoured the former, the doctrine of
philosophical necessity must always be clearly distinguished
from the Calvinistic, religious, understanding of bondage and
predestination.[51] He quotes from Calvin's *De Libero Arbitrio*
by way of underlining the point: 'If liberty is opposed to
coaction (or force) I confess and constantly assert that the
will is free, and I reckon him a heretic who thinks otherwise.
If it is called free in this sense, — because it is not forced or
violently drawn by an external movement, but is led on *sua
sponte,* I have no objection to this. But because men in
general, when they hear this epithet applied to the will of
man understand it in a very different sense, for this reason I
dislike it.'[52] Not all critics have been silenced by such assertion, however, and the Anglican Cunningham persists in thinking that Calvin fails to follow Augustine in that 'he does not
appear to see the importance of voluntariness in our action as
bearing on responsibility, and he uses language which seems
to make the Divine control over the human consciousness so
complete as to remove the decision in cases of sin from the
mind of man to the mind of God — as when he notes without
any attempt at qualification how God "directs men's counsels,
and excites their wills, and regulates their efforts as He
pleases". It is difficult to reconcile such language with any
sort of human responsibility'.[53] For the other side, Warfield
insists that there is 'nothing against which Calvinism sets its
face with more firmness than every form and degree of auto-
soterism'.[54] God's grace alone is able to save.

    In such exchanges as those just cited we see the polarisation
of views. Those on the evangelical Arminian wing never ceased
to protest against what they took to be the reduction of the
God and Father of our Lord Jesus Christ to an absolute,
capricious, inscrutable will, from whose deliberations even the
Son is excluded. Those on the Calvinist side were ever concerned to adopt what they considered to be accurate views of
man's state — views which required sovereign grace as the only
possible remedy — and to ascribe *all* the glory of salvation to
God.

    So much for man's plight and man's will. What, now, of
the Godward aspects of the debate? The classical statement
of Calvin's teaching on election is as follows:

'In actual fact the covenant of life is not preached equally among all men, and among those to whom it is preached, it does not gain the same acceptance either constantly or in equal degree. In this diversity the wonderful depth of God's judgment is made known. For there is no doubt that this variety also serves the decision of God's eternal election.'[55]

There follows a cautionary word concerning undue speculation in this field, and a disquisition upon the scriptural doctrine of election. Calvin concludes:

'As Scripture, then, clearly shows, we say that God once established by his eternal and unchangeable plan those whom he long before determined once for all to receive into salvation, and those whom, on the other hand, he would devote to destruction. We assert that, with respect to the elect, this plan was founded upon his freely given mercy, without regard to human worth; but by his just and irreprehensible but incomprehensible judgment he has barred the door of life to those whom he has given over to damnation.'[56]

There are clear Augustinian echoes here, though it should be noted that whereas for Augustine baptism regenerates, to Calvin the regenerating agent is the Spirit of God working through the Word; and further, that while Augustine inclines towards infralapsarianism, Calvin inclines towards supralapsarianism. For all that, Calvin throws the emphasis upon election to salvation, and treats the decree of reprobation with wholesome reserve. With similar delicacy the framers of the Westminster Confession were later to eschew the term 'reprobation'. They preferred to speak of the predestination of the elect, and of the foreordination of those who were to be passed by (preterition). Reprobation is not, of course, deemed to flout the love of God, for he could, with equal justice have condemned the whole race of fallen man. The reprobate, in fact, glorify God by testifying to his justice. But as to why these and not those are foreordained to reprobation — here we may not pry, but must simply and humbly refer to God's inscrutable wisdom. We may be sure that the cause is 'just though unknown'.[57] God no more saves because of merits than he damns because of demerits. We are to 'seek no cause out-

side his will'.[58] (Clearly, undue emphasis upon this type of
Calvin's statements leads directly to Beza, and thence to the
'iron will' view of God).

The Arminians were to protest vehemently against what
they understood to be this unworthy view of God — unworthy
because it was unethical. Arminius himself, as we have seen,
and the early Remonstrants, softened the doctrine of the
decrees by substituting 'foreknowledge' for 'predestination'.
The decrees thus became conditional, and this in the interests
of God's justice and (later) man's freedom and responsibility.
To the Calvinists, however, this was to place God at man's
disposal in a quite intolerable manner; indeed, it was to make
the sure salvation of *any* impossible to assert, thereby undermining the doctrine of God's omnipotence: 'A decree or purpose, based or founded solely upon the foreknowledge of
foresight of the faith and obedience of individuals, is, of
course, the same thing as the entire want or non-existence of
any purpose or decree in regard to them. It determines
nothing concerning them, — bestows nothing upon them, —
secures nothing to them.'[59] Further, although the charge could
not be levelled at Arminius himself, 'Arminians are accustomed
to identify the election of a particular individual with his
faith or believing in Christ, as if there were no antecedent act
of God bearing upon him . . . until he believed; while others
of them . . . identify the time of God's decree of election
with the death of believers, as if then only their salvation
became by the event certain, or certainly known, while till
that time nothing had been done to effect or secure it'.[60] The
Calvinists, on the contrary, claimed that if the foreknower is
God, then since he can foreknow only what *will* occur (for he
is not liable to error), the assertion of *his* foreknowledge is
tantamount to the assertion of predestination and foreordination. Otherwise, once again, God is dependent upon man for
the final outcome of his plans. Moreover, if men are required
to have the faith which the Arminians claim God foresees that
they will have, this is a denial of the truth that God is the
true and only author of salvation. To the Calvinist the truth
is that 'Whatever He decrees He effects, and this agreed with
His omnipotence. His will is joined with His power, constitut-
ing a symmetry worthy of that providence which governs all

things'.[61] It follows that, *pace* Arminianism, God's grace is irresistible; it also follows — Arminius's hesitation, and some of his followers' denials notwithstanding — that the saints cannot but persevere. This is all the result of the Spirit's work. The notion of man's co-operation with God's grace as being the means to salvation completely misses the mark, and affords no explanation of the believer's state and hope.[62]

The Arminian ethical protest cannot easily be set aside, however, and it has seldom been so forcibly expressed as by Aubrey Moore: 'Calvinism is not accidentally but essentially immoral, since it makes the distinction between right and wrong a matter of positive enactment, and thereby makes it possible to assert that what is immoral of man is moral for God, because He is above morality.'[63] The Calvinists would reply that they do not hold more than that what *appears* immoral to men may be moral to God — but this still leaves us with the question whether or not Calvinism inevitably leaves us in the last resort with the inscrutable will of God, to which all perplexities of the kind just stated are referred. Certainly Calvin feels that he is being entirely faithful to the scriptures in his predestinarian teaching, but many, with Dr. Whale, would avow that 'the unflinching logic of double pre-destination is not typical of Scripture taken as a whole. The Bible nowhere directly asserts the *decretum horribile*'.[64] It is precisely this which has made many declare that in the last resort Calvin's God is will, not love. Some have gone so far as to charge him with a pantheism not far removed from Spinoza's. Fairbairn, for example, argues that 'Calvin was as pure, though not as conscious and consistent a Pantheist as Spinoza . . . Calvin may be said to have anticipated Spinoza in his notion of God as *causa immanens*'.[65] To which accusation Warfield made what seems to us to be a quite satisfactory reply:

'when the Calvinist spoke of God as the *prima causa rerum* . . . he meant by it only that all that takes place takes place in accordance with the divine will, not that the divine will is the only efficient cause in the universe; and when Calvin quotes approvingly from Augustine . . . that "the will of God is the necessity of things", so little is either he or Augustine making use of the words in a Pantheistic

sense that he hastens to explain that what he means is only
that whatever God has willed will certainly come to pass,
although it comes to pass in "such a manner that the cause
and matter of it are found in" the second causes (*ut causa
et materia in ipsis reperiatur*).'[66]

Again, the will of God is not a capricious will to the
Calvinist: it is a holy and a just will. Yet lingering doubts
remain, and our suggestion is that perhaps, like Augustine,
Calvin does not adequately relate Christ and his saving work
to the concept of the decrees. It is not that Christ is *not* there
in the *Institutes* and elsewhere; it is manifest that double predestination *is* there; it is that they are not related entirely
satisfactorily (and we grant that human limitation will for
ever prevent complete harmonisation). For Calvin, Christ is
the mirror of predestination, for he was honoured as God's
Son solely by God's election and quite apart from his merits;[67]
but as Professor Reid says, 'this is not to secure for Christ a
place in the framing of that divine purpose to election . . .
for the primary ground of Predestination, we have to penetrate
into the *divinae sapientiae adyta,* where we find it lodged in
an *arcanum consilium.* And it appears that into these deep
counsels, Christ has not been admitted . . . This . . . is the
fundamental reason why [Calvin] can relate the elect and the
reprobate identically to the will of God'.[68] Precisely because
the character of God-in-Christ appears to be underplayed in
the Trinitarian redemption transaction, we are left with a God
who can *as willingly* consign his creatures to one final destiny
as to the other. James Orr expresses both the worth of
Calvinism, and the sense of uneasiness which some statements
of it foster:

'Calvin exalts the sovereignty of God, and this is right. But
he errs in placing his root-idea of God in sovereign will
rather than in love. Love is subordinated to sovereignty,
instead of sovereignty to love . . . I do not, therefore,
abate one whit from the sovereignty of God in the election,
calling, and salvation of such as are saved; but I do feel
strongly that this election of God must not be disjoined
from the context in which it is set in God's historical
purpose, which, grounded in His love, embraces the widest
possible ultimate blessing for the whole world. I hold as

strongly as Augustine or Calvin that only as God chooses men will they ever choose him . . . but if God's method is thus necessarily one of election, it is in order that in each soul saved He may set up a new centre . . . from which He may work with greater effect for the accomplishment of wider ends.'[69]

Whilst accepting this statement as far as it goes we respectfully suggest that it requires to be strengthened still further by the realisation that God calls not simply individuals, but *a people* for his praise.

On balance we feel that an amelioration of Calvinism is to be preferred to a capitulation to Arminian extremes. The judicious William Ames (1576—1633) may speak for us in his suitably qualified way: 'The view of the Remonstrants, as it is taken by the mass of their supporters, is not strictly a heresy, but a dangerous error tending towards heresy. As maintained by some of them, however, it is the Pelagian heresy: because they deny that the effective operation of inward grace is necessary for conversion.'[70] Further complaint against Calvinism, to the effect that it leads towards evangelistic lethargy and to antinomianism will come to the fore in the ensuing debate, as will such complaints against Arminianism as that its universalism and perfectionism respectively minimise God's justice and man's sin, and unduly exalt fallen man's ethical ability.

CHAPTER TWO

Some Tributaries

Through the zeal, not to mention the continental commuting, of John Knox (1505—72)[1] Calvinism soon made its impact upon Scotland. Not indeed that he was its only champion, but he was, by common consent, pre-eminent. We must resist the temptation to expand on the history of the Scottish Reformation, and confine ourselves to the particular doctrinal debate which concerns us: that concerning the nature and relations of God and man.

Knox's *Treatise on Predestination,* written in 1559, was published in Geneva in 1560. It is, to quote its subtitle, *An Answer to a great number of Blasphemous Cavillations written by an Anabaptist and Adversarie to God's Eternal Predestination . . .,* and in it he upholds the divine sovereignty, maintains human inability to perform any sinless act, and ascribes salvation exclusively to God's electing grace. The year 1560 also saw the publication of the Scots Confession, which remained the sole standard of the Scottish Reformed Church until the Westminster Confession replaced it in 1647. In Dr. Donald MacLean's lyrical words, 'The Scots Confession, under which the Church for eighty-seven formative years fought her battles, won her victories, moulded the theology and the character of a nation, and inspired a people with religious enthusiasm, was produced, with unparalleled quickness, in four days.'[2] The work of the 'six Johns': Willock, Spottiswoode, Douglas, Row, Winram and Knox, it is generally conceded that it is the spirit of the last named which most obviously permeates it. It is asserted that 'The spirit of the Lord Jesus dwelling in us by faith brings forth good works', and it is noteworthy that whereas predestination to election is affirmed, there is no specific reference to reprobation. The

following statement from the section on Faith in the Holy
Ghost is of particular relevance to our discussion:

> 'Our faith and its assurance do not proceed from flesh and
> blood, that is to say, from natural powers within us, but
> are the inspiration of the Holy Ghost . . . For by nature we
> are so dead, blind, and perverse, that neither can we feel
> when we are pricked, see the light when it shines, nor
> assent to the will of God when it is revealed, unless the
> Spirit of the Lord Jesus quicken that which is dead, remove
> the darkness from our minds, and bow our stubborn hearts
> to the obedience of His blessed will . . . To put this even
> more plainly; as we willingly disclaim any honour and glory
> for our own creation and redemption, so do we willingly also
> for our regeneration and sanctification . . .'[3]

A further Confession of Faith, devised by the Assembly of
Aberdeen in 1616, revealed no relaxation in respect of things
Calvinistic,[4] and Walter Balcanquhal (1586?–1645), episcopalian Dean of Ross and Calvinist, attended the Synod of Dort
at the behest of James I.

Meanwhile in England a line of Anglican Calvinists, some of
them more moderate than others, was on the point of being
followed by Arminian successors. In addition to William
Perkins and his Arminian opponent Peter Baro, to whom we
have already referred, the Calvinists included Matthew Parker
(1504–75), Archbishop of Canterbury, under whom Convoca-
tion, in 1562, approved the Thirty-nine Articles (which were
derived from the Forty-two Articles of 1553); Edmund
Grindal (1519?–83), Archbishop of Canterbury; John Jewel
(1522–71), Bishop of Salisbury and apologist for the anti-
quity of the Church of England;[5] John Whitgift (1544–1600)
and Richard Bancroft (1544–1610), two further Archbishops
of Canterbury, of whom the former censured Samuel Harsnett
for preaching against absolute predestination in 1584, and
chaired the committee which drew up the nine (supralapsarian) Lambeth Articles of 1595. The increasing vogue of
Arminianism is amply demonstrated by the elevation to high
office of these successors to those just named: William Laud
(1573–1645), Archbishop of Canterbury; Jeremy Taylor
(1613–67), Bishop of Down and Connor who, though chiefly

and rightly remembered for his poetry, and for such devotional works as *The Rule and Exercise of Holy Living* (1650) and *The Rule and Exercise of Holy Dying* (1651), also provoked controversy with his allegedly Pelagianising tract *Unum Necessarium* (1655), which was said to undermine the doctrine of original sin; William Sancroft (1617—93), Archbishop of Canterbury; and George Bull (1634—1710), Bishop of St. David's. We do not wish to suggest that matters were tidier than in fact they were. Calvinism within the Anglican fold did not entirely retreat before Arminianism. Thus, for example, in 1615, when Laud was in his forties, the Irish Church under Professor (later Archbishop) Ussher (1581—1656) adopted a set of Calvinistic articles; and about 1624 the King's chaplain, Richard Montague, was accused by Parliament and by four bishops including Carleton, a Dort deputy, and Ussher, of reviving the teaching of Baro and denying the doctrine of perseverance in his work *Appeal to Caesar*.[6] But there can be no denying the cordial reception which an increasing number of clergy gave to Arminianism. The Free Churchman Fairbairn suggests that these Arminians adopted their theology not simply because of an aversion to Calvinism, but because their high church polity, resting as it did upon the idea of the divine right of kings and bishops was easier to sustain under a conditional theology than it would have been under a theology which uncompromisingly exalted God's sovereignty.[7] The Anglicans we have mentioned were in some respects the forerunners of the eighteenth century Latitudinarians, though the latter — not to mention Arminius himself — would have scorned their sacramentarianism. It is not without significance that Anglican interest in Arminian teaching arose at the time of the arrival in England in 1613 of Grotius (1583—1645), to whom we shall return shortly.

Turning now to the English dissenters we note first the General or Arminian Baptists. Their founder was John Smyth (c. 1554—1612), who had been at Cambridge during the Perkins—Baro controversy, and who in 1609 founded the first English Baptist church. Significantly, he did this while in exile on Dutch soil, at the time of the debate over Arminius's views, and in proximity to the Mennonites, by whom he was influenced. Smyth held that God 'predestinated all men to

life, reprobating nobody', and that by virtue of his possession
of free-will, man is able to mortify his sins, whereupon
Christ's death becomes efficacious.[8] In their 1678 Confession
the General Baptists asserted that 'Christ died for all men,
and there is a sufficiency in his death and merits for the sins
of the whole world . . . [he] hath sent forth his spirit to
accompany the word in order to beget repentance and faith
. . .'.[9] Smyth's colleague Thomas Helwys (c. 1550–c. 1616),
who on returning to England formed the first English
Baptist church on English soil – at Spitalfields – in 1612,
though he broke from Smyth on the questions of toleration
and ecclesiastical succession, never relinquished his
Arminianism, as witness his work, *A Short and Plaine Proof
. . . that God's Decree is not the Cause of anye Mans Sinne or
Condemnation: and that all Men are redeemed by Christ; as
also That no Infants are Condemned* (1611).[10]

All of this was in marked contrast to the sturdy Calvinism
of the Particular Baptist Confessions of 1644 (the work of
Londoners), 1655 (Warwick), and 1656 (Wessex); and of the
(largely Presbyterian) Westminster Confession of Faith (1646),
and its revisions: the (Independent) Savoy Declaration of
Faith and Order (1658), and the Particular Baptist Confession
of 1677 (further revised in 1689). Among the more impressive
theologians at Westminster were the supralapsarians William
Twisse (1578?–1646) and William Prynne (1600–69); John
Owen (1616–83) was prominent at the Savoy. There were
significant differences between these confessions – and this
not only in connection with matters of church government.
Into some of these we shall shortly enquire.

It is somewhat surprising, in view of the stand of the General
Baptists, that Bishop Burnet (1643–1715) should have
thought that John Goodwin (1593–1665),[11] who was not
yet twenty when Smyth died, 'first brought in Arminianism
among the sectaries'.[12] Educated at Erasmus's College, Queen's
Cambridge, Goodwin became Vicar of St. Stephen's Coleman
Street. He was ejected by the Committee of Plundered
Ministers in 1645, ostensibly because he refused to practise
indiscriminate baptism, and to admit all parishioners to
communion. What really grieved his opponents, however, was
his Arminianism, which the Presbyterians hated, and his

republicanism, which made him anathema to the high church episcopalians. He thus became an Independent minister in his former parish. To say that one was either for Goodwin or against him is to put it mildly. To a certain Mr. Granger Goodwin 'made more noise in the world than any other person of his age, rank, and profession';[13] and Thomas Edwards (1599—1647) vilified him in his *Gangraena* (1646) as 'a monstrous sectary, a compound of Socinianism, Arminianism, Libertinism, Antinomianism, Independency, Popery, yea and of Scepticism . . .'.[14] Goodwin was more than competent in pugilistic letters, and published his reply. *Cretensis : or, a brief Answer to an ulcerous Treatise . . .* in the following year. More soberly, he set down his view of the crucial doctrines in the debate. He held

> 'That Christ died for the sins of all mankind; that the benefits of his death were intended for all; and that natural men may do such things as whereunto God has by way of promise annexed grace and acceptation . . . That man hath a free-will and power in himself to repent, to believe, to obey the gospel, and do every thing that God requires to salvation.'[15]

These doctrines were among a catalogue of Goodwin's alleged errors published by a group of London clergy meeting at Sion College on 14th December 1647; and undeniably Goodwin was of the opinion that 'The necessity and power of those tenets or doctrines, nick-named *Arminian,* is so great for the accommodating and promoting the affairs of Christianity, that even those persons themselves who get a good part of their subsistence in the world by decrying them, and declaiming against them, yet cannot make earnings of their profession, are not able to carry on their work of preaching, with any tolerable satisfaction to those that hear them, without employing and asserting them very frequently'.[16]

Few attacked the seventeenth century version of Arminianism so earnestly as the ejected Christopher Ness (1621—1705) who, in his *An Antidote Against Arminianism* (1700), proceeds through the Arminian points in a manner which blends the scholastic method with evangelical zeal, and, for good measure, adds a dash of the then fashionable abuse.

Thus, he enquires, 'What are the new Arminians but the varnished offspring of the old Pelagians, that makes the grace of God to lacquey it at the foot, or rather, the will of man?'.[17] Among many fuller defences of Calvinism against Arminianism is Elisha Coles's *A Practical Discourse of God's Sovereignty* (1673), which was in its fourteenth edition by 1768, and which has exceeded fifty editions to date. Among those who have written commendations of the work are Thomas Goodwin (1600–80), John Owen, and Samuel Annesley (1620?–96).[18] Few were as adept as Thomas Watson (c. 1620–1686) at bringing out what were taken to be the *religious* defects of Arminianism. Thus, for example, on perseverance he writes,

> 'How despairing is the Arminian doctrine of falling from grace! To-day a saint, to-morrow a reprobate; to-day a Peter, to-morrow a Judas. This must needs cut the sinews of a Christian's endeavour, and be like boring a hole in a vessel: to make all the wine of his joy run out . . . What comfort were it to have one's name written in the book of life, if it might be blotted out again? But be assured, for your comfort, grace, if true, though never so weak, shall persevere. Though a Christian has but little grace to trade with, yet he need not fear breaking, because God not only gives him a stock of grace, but will keep his stock for him. *Gratia concutitur, non excutitur.* Augustine. "Grace may be shaken with fears and doubts, but it cannot be plucked up by the roots" '.[19]

As well as the Arminian criticism of Calvinism there were also attempts to modify the latter made by those who were more generally sympathetic with it. We shall first note Amyraldism and its derivatives, and then federalism. Amyraldism takes its name from Moise Amyraut (1596–1664), the most eminent disciple of John Cameron (1579–1625) who, before being appointed Principal of the University of Glasgow, taught from 1618–21 in the Protestant Faculty of the seminary at Saumur.[20] Cameron, seeking a *via media* between the Calvinism of Dort and its Arminian opponent, thought he had found it in the position which came to be known as hypothetical universalism. His aim was to restore the concept of predestination to the place Calvin's *Institutes* had given it, rather than to make it the first premise of a scholastic dogmatic structure. At the same time he wished to avoid the Pelagianising possibilities inherent in Arminianism. His approach was pursued by Amyraut, who taught that whereas the atonement was universal in its scope, and thus adequate to the needs of God's antecedent decree of salvation, it was effectual only in the case of the elect. God foresaw that, because of sin, not all would in fact believe, and he therefore decreed to elect some. The difficulty with this position was its tendency to bifurcate in either of two opposed directions: into Arminianism by virtue of the emphasis upon the universally provided atonement; or into Calvinism because of the realisation that man's inability required God's electing grace. Moreover, it was all too easy to reopen the crucial wound by asking 'Who makes the hypothetical reference actual – God, or man?'. Amyraut's development of the Dort position to the effect that since Christ died sufficiently for all though effectually only for the elect, there was an external call addressed to the pious heathen, caused further consternation in the Calvinist ranks. Among the factors which motivated Amyraut was the hope that his position might make Reformed teaching more acceptable to the Lutherans. He failed in this, but managed to avoid condemnation by the Synod of the French Reformed Church in 1637.

Two other Saumur professors caused ecclesiastical concern: Claude Pajon (1626–1685), who was accused of Pelagianising, and was condemned in 1677; and Josue de la Place (1592–1632), who taught the mediate, rather than the immediate, imputation of Adam's sin. This view was denounced by the Synod of Charenton in 1645 and when, with the revocation of the Edict of Nantes (18th October 1685) Huguenot refugees began to make their way to the Netherlands, the Walloon Synod required an anti-Amyraldian subscription of all in-coming ministers.[21] Amyraldism was supported by Daillé and Blondel, and vigorously opposed by Rivet and Spanheim and, above all, by Francis Turretin (1671–1737).

Few in England gave Amyraldism so cordial a reception as Richard Baxter (1615–91).[22] He wrote, 'I should think it a great benefit if I had the opportunity of sitting at the feet of

so judicious a man as I perceiv Amyraldus to bee'.[23] Baxter
was one who adopted a mediating position in theology not
out of apathy, or in an attempt to curry favour with pro-
ponents on either side, or in order to befuddle the simple, but
out of conviction. Indeed, the middle position in this debate
was not at all a comfortable one, and Baxter found it
necessary to fire broadsides to the right and to the left — as
witness his attack on Crispian antinomianism (of which more
anon) on the one hand, and his criticisms of his fellow
Cromwellian chaplain, Peter Sterry (1613—72), and his defence
of the Arminian John Goodwin on the other. Baxter charged
Sterry with advocating that 'mixture of Platonisme,
Origenisme, and Arianisme which was more rational than
scriptural'.[24] Baxter genuinely saw the necessity of good
works, the importance of reason, the need of an experimental
faith, and the unalterable priority of grace. In his *Catholic
Theology* (1675) he presented the fullest statement of his
theological position. He contends for the view that God's
predestinating decree has reference only to the elect and not
to the reprobate. Salvation depends upon Christ's righteousness, by which he fulfilled the old law and inaugurated the
new; and upon man's faithful and repentant obedience to the
new law's demands. Man's competence to obey the new law
(the emphasis upon which gave the name 'Neonomianism' to
Baxter's position) is derived from the Holy Spirit, whose
grace the elect enjoy more fully than others. This increase of
grace ensures that some *will* be saved. On the other hand,
men may render saving grace ineffectual by resisting it — at
which point John Owen demurred. In urging that what is
imputed to man with a view to justification is not Christ's
righteousness but, rather, man's faith in Christ's righteousness, Baxter was setting his face against that antinomianism
which, he thought, removed man ultimately from the sphere
of moral agency altogether. The manner in which Baxter
expresses his belief in Christ's compliance with, and replace-
ment of, the old law, thereby becoming the head of God's
government, reveals his indebtedness to the Arminian Grotius
who in his *Defence of the Catholic Faith concerning the
Satisfaction of Christ against Socinus* (1617), suggested that
Christ does not so much expiate past sins by bearing the

penalty, as perform the role of exemplar-deterrent in respect of future sins. On all of which James Orr commented, 'The weakness of this theory plainly lies in its reduction of the atonement from something rendered necessary by the essential relation of God to the sinner, to the level of a rectoral device, having no ground in essential justice, but intended only to produce an *impression* on the mind of the beholder'.[25] In a word, the tendency in governmentalism is to teach that the law is dealt with by being *replaced*; in orthodox Calvinism the law is dealt with by being *fulfilled*.

If Baxter welcomed Amyraldism, the same could not be said of Cameron's compatriot, Samuel Rutherford (1600– 61).[26] Positively, Rutherford stoutly maintained the supra-lapsarian position, and when we reflect on the possibility that so important a figure as Dr. Strang, Principal of Glasgow College, had to relinquish his position because he veered (only) so far as infralapsarianism,[27] we may well understand why Fairbairn should assert of Cameron that 'he preferred the freedom of the French to the bondage of the Scotch Church'.[28] On more than one occasion Rutherford was invited to take up an academic post in the Netherlands where, although the infralapsarianism of Johannes Cocceius (1603–69) was in the ascendant, the supralapsarianism of his opponent Gisbert Voetius (1589–1676) was also influential. In common with other supralapsarians Rutherford did not shrink from locating the decrees of election and reprobation in the absolutely sovereign will of God. This was asserted in the interests of God's freedom. That is, it was not deemed proper to suggest that God could not have saved except by the way of Christ's atonement. But, as Principal MacLeod points out, although Rutherford (and his mentor in these matters, Twisse) did not deviate from this position, John Owen, who had been in agreement with Rutherford, 'came to see his mistake, and in his defence of Punitive Justice as rooted not in the bare will but in the very nature of God . . . has left what one might call the classical work of British Theology dealing with the subject'.[29] Negatively, Rutherford hotly denounced Arminianism, and in this connection Dr. Walker has delight-fully and accurately summed him up thus:

'Rutherford was somewhat of a hero-worshipper, and his

heroes were the schoolmen, Bradwardine (Magnus
Bradwardine he always called him), and the Puritan Dr.
Twiss. His choice of masters was not a happy one; and he
seems to have contracted from them a certain scholastic
artificiality. At the same time, it is impossible not to
admire the marvellous keenness of his mind, and the alert-
ness with which he flashes through that maze of logical
distinctions, now crossing swords with Bellarmine, now
striking hard at Suarez, now, as he thinks, laying Arminius
low. I have sometimes fancied that his Latin went on with
a more vigorous and jubilant tread when the difficulties
and intricacies are the greatest.'[30]

Rutherford had no patience with Arminian tendencies to
universalism. He doughtily championed the limited atonement
doctrine, holding that while Christ's death was intrinsically
adequate to effect satisfaction for the sins of all, this was
not his purpose, and hence he did not do it. It remains only
to add that Rutherford did not confine his anti-Arminian
onslaughts to his more theological works. In one sermon, for
example, he concludes with answers to nine Arminian objections.[31] Not that he had any patience with that antinomian
error to which some of his Calvinistic colleagues were,
doctrinally if not practically, prone. In one paragraph he
castigates his two foes thus:

'When either grace is turned into painted, but rotten
nature, as Arminians do, or into wantonness, as others do,
the error to me is of a far other and higher elevation, than
opinions touching church government. Tenacious adhering
to Antinomian errors, with an obstinate and final persistence
in them, both as touching faith to, and suitable practice of
them, I shall think, cannot be fathered upon any of the
regenerated; for it is an opinion not in the margin and
borders, but in the page and body, and too near the centre
and vital parts of the gospel.'[32]

Among the lesser man who sided with Rutherford was John
Brown of Wamphray (1610?–1679), whose *The Life of
Justification Opened,* an attack upon Baxterianism, was
published in 1695.[33] Later men in Rutherford's line included
Robert Traill (1642–1716)[34] who, as well as participating in

the antinomian controversy,[35] prepared Rutherford's *Examini
Arminianismi* (1668) for the press after his master's death. It
is neither difficult nor far-fetched to see an allusion to Baxter
in Traill's view that 'the middle way betwixt the "Arminians"
and the "Orthodox", had been espoused, and strenuously
defended and promoted, by some Nonconformists, of great
note for piety and parts; and usually such men that are for
middle ways in points of doctrine, have a greater kindness for
that extreme they go halfway to, than for that which they go
halfway from'.[36] As for Arminianism itself, Traill is persuaded
that its principles are 'the natural dictates of a carnal mind
. . . and, next to the dead sea of Popery (into which also this
stream runs), have, since Pelagius to this day, been the
greatest plague of the Church of Christ . . .'.[37]

For all their differences in detail from each other, and
from Rutherford, Baxter and the later Owen were united in
their allegiance to a version of the federal theology. Among
the difficulties in dealing with federalism is the fact that
W. Adams Brown's desire, expressed in 1904, to see an adequate account of the origin and history of the covenant
theology, still awaits fulfilment.[38] Brown urges the necessity
of distinguishing between the covenant idea as found in
scripture, and the covenant or federal theology which was
erected upon it. He explains that the Calvinist theologians
who espoused the theory regarded it as providing the frame-
work of thought within which they could accommodate not
only their belief concerning the believer's ground of assurance,
but also their ecclesiology, their ethics, and their understanding of history. We are here concerned with the first only
of these.

In its bare bones (and there are many enfleshments of it)
the federal theology, which amounts to a theory of immediate
imputation, asserts that God freely condescended to approach
man by way of a covenant. In the words of the Westminster
Confession:

'The distance between God and the creature is so great,
that although reasonable creatures do owe obedience unto
him as their Creator, yet they could never have any fruition
of him as their blessedness and reward, but by some

voluntary condescension on God's part, which he hath been pleased to express by way of a covenant.

The first covenant made with man was a covenant of works, wherein life was promised to Adam, and in him to his posterity, upon condition of perfect and personal obedience.

Man by his fall having made himself incapable of life by that covenant, the Lord was pleased to make a second, commonly called the Covenant of Grace: whereby he freely offereth unto sinners life and salvation by Jesus Christ, requiring of them faith in him, that they may be saved; and promising to give unto all those that are ordained unto life his Holy Spirit, to make them willing and able to believe . . . under the law [this covenant] was administered by promises, prophecies, sacrifices, circumcision, the paschal lamb, and other types and ordinances . . . Under the gospel . . . the ordinances in which this covenant is dispensed are the preaching of the word, and the administration of the sacraments of Baptism and the Lord's Supper . . . There are not therefore two covenants of grace . . . but one and the same under various dispensations.'[39]

It is noteworthy that this Confession (which, alone among the Reformed confessions — with the exception of the Formula Consensus Helvetica — embodies the classical statement of the federal viewpoint) appeared in 1647, one year before Cocceius's work on the subject was published. For all that, Cocceius is often designated as founder of the system.[40] In fact, however, there appear to be two main streams of thought which converged in developed federalism. One was German, the other was British (we use the term advisedly). Associated with the former were Caspar Olevianus (1536–1587) and Zacharius Ursinus (1534–1583) and others.[41] In 1596 Olevianus published the *Expositio Symboli,* and in 1585 there appeared his great work *De substantia foederis gratuiti inter Deum et electos itenque de mediis* . . . For him 'covenant' is synonymous with 'church' and 'kingdom', and he thinks exclusively in terms of a covenant of grace. His followers, among them Eglin and Martinius pressed the idea of the covenant into the pre-fall period, and upheld the existence of the two covenants — those of grace and works. Although

Olevianus and Ursinus were among those who drew up the Heidelberg Catechism (1563) their covenant ideas did not find expression therein. Among the abler federal theologians was Hermann Witsius (1636–1708), whose *De Oeconomia foederum Dei cum hominibus* (1677) was influential both on the continent and in the Anglo-Saxon world — the fact that some of his fellow federalists accused him of having sinned against the Holy Ghost notwithstanding.

From the British side came Robert Rollock (1555?–98), Principal of the University of Edinburgh. In his *Quaestiones et Responsiones aliquot de foedere Dei deque Sacramento quod foederis Dei sigillum est* (1596) he discoursed upon the mutual relations of covenant and sacrament. William Ames (1576–1633), author of the *Marrow of Sacred Divinity* (1642), maintained the *foedus operum,* and, when in exile in Holland during the reign of James I, numbered Cocceius amongst his pupils. *A Treatise of the Covenant of Grace* by John Ball (1585–1640) was published posthumously in 1642, and Ussher's covenant doctrine was expounded in his *Body of Divinity* (1645), and in the Irish Articles to which we earlier referred. We ought in passing to recall that the covenant concept was by no means simply a matter of theological convenience to those who embraced it. To some it was a matter of life and death — as the history of Scotland, for example, shows. In 1581 an appendix to the Scots Confession of 1560 was subscribed to. It took the form of a national covenant. Later, in 1638, David Dickson (1583?–1663)[42] addressed the Glasgow Assembly on the advantages of the federal theology and the perils of Arminianism. He was the author of *Truth's Victory over Error,* the first commentary on the Westminster Confession of Faith. Dickson further co-operated with James Durham in writing the covenant-centred work *The Sum of Saving Knowledge,* for so long a popular compendium of theology in Scotland; and his liturgical interests were reflected in the *Directory for Public Worship* which he compiled jointly with Alexander Henderson and David Calderwood.

The Arminians were not without their own understanding of 'covenant'. Thus, Arminius himself thought of God's condescending covenant relationship with man under two aspects. There was, in the first place, 'a law placed in and imprinted

on the mind of man; in which is contained his natural duty
towards God and his neighbour, and therefore towards himself also . . .'.[43] Secondly, there was a symbolical law, that
is, 'one that prescribes or forbids some act, which in itself
is neither agreeable nor disagreeable to God, that is, one that
is indifferent: And it serves for this purpose, that God may
try whether man is willing to yield obedience to Him solely
on this account, — because it has been the pleasure of God to
require such obedience, and though it were impossible to
devise any other reason why God imposed that law'.[44] The
obedience yielded to the latter is far inferior to that yielded
to the former — indeed, it is 'not so much *obedience itself* as
the external profession of willingly yielding obedience . . .'.[45]
The Calvinists, of course, recognised no such distinction in
the motives for obedience to God's will: it was his will, and
that was enough. Some followers of Arminius went further in
this as in other matters. They suggested that when Adam fell
the legal covenant was set aside, and God graciously instituted
his covenant of grace, whereby he condescended to accept faith
in Christ as fulfiller of the law in lieu of obedience to the
law itself. Moreover, some deemed it unreasonable to expect
fallen man to render proper obedience to God, especially
since he had forfeited enabling grace. The Calvinistic reply to
the latter point was that 'ought' does not imply 'can'; that
the demands of the law remain; that to minimise these is to do
violence to God's righteousness; and that man alone is
responsible for violating them. As to the former point, the
Calvinists regarded this as reducing faith to a work, and
Robert Traill returned the characteristic verdict when he said
that 'Faith in Jesus Christ doth justify . . . only as a mere
instrument receiving that imputed righteousness of Christ, for
which we are justified; and that this faith, in the office of
justification, is neither condition nor qualification, nor our
gospel-righteousness, but in its very act a renouncing of all
such pretences'.[46] That is, salvation is of the Lord *alone*. As
A. A. Hodge much later put it, 'Faith is not a work which
Christ condescends in the gospel to accept instead of perfect
obedience as the ground of salvation — it is only the hand
whereby we clasp the person and work of our Redeemer, which
is the true ground of salvation'.[47]

There are some grounds for thinking that the Savoy Declaration is even more federally oriented than the Westminster Confession. This, at any rate, is the contention of Dr. Toon.[48] He supports his view by referring to the question of repentance, *inter alia.* Whereas the Westminster divines 'described repentance primarily from the human point of view as a responsibility of man to God, the Savoy divines chose to view it in the light of God's eternal purposes and of federal theology, and therefore as a gift of God to His elect'.[49] With this we may agree; but when Dr. Toon proceeds to imply that Savoy's new chapter XX 'Of the Gospel, and of the extent of the Grace thereof', over-emphasises 'God's love to the *elect* in the eternal covenant of grace',[50] we beg to differ. At best the evidence of the text is ambiguous. Dr. Toon quotes from the first and third sections of the chapter, the first of which does appear somewhat restrictive, for the *elect* are specified as the recipients of repentance and faith. But is it clear from the words of section iii which Dr. Toon quotes: 'The revelation of the Gospel unto sinners . . . is merely of the sovereign will and good pleasure of God . . .' that the gospel invitation or call is restricted? For the term 'sinners' stands unqualified and may therefore be understood extensively.[51] Furthermore, had Dr. Toon continued to the end of section iii he would have found those very words which to Dr. W. T. Whitley constituted the evidence of genuine evangelical concern on the part of the Savoy divines: 'In all ages the Preaching of the Gospel hath been granted unto persons and nations, as to the extent and straitning of it, in great variety, according to the counsel of the will of God.'[52]

Our hesitation concerning some details of Dr. Toon's argument notwithstanding, we *do* detect stronger federalist overtones in the Declaration than in the Confession. But when Dr. Toon concludes that the Savoy divines 'sincerely emphasised the sovereign grace of God not realising they were tipping the balances too much on one side and therefore omitting or weakening an essential element in Holy Scripture, namely the responsibility of men to God',[53] we have to ask two questions: did they thus demean man? Did they realise they were doing it? As to the former, whilst we should not expect to find the Savoy divines tending towards Arminianism, we need look no further than chapter XIX of the Declaration if we would find human responsibility writ large. There the continuing force of the moral law is underlined, its uses are stipulated, and its fulfilment is enjoined upon men. As to the latter, even if the Savoy divines demeaned man more than we think they did, then on the assumption that one should think twice before appearing to patronise such intellects as those of John Owen and some of his colleagues, we would simply say that it is at least as reasonable to speculate that they knew what they were doing and, in face of Arminian and sectarian opponents, thought the risk worth taking.

Undeniably John Owen was influential in giving Savoy its federal cast, but when Dr. Toon in his generally useful book on Owen considers Dr. Perry Miller's view that the Puritans employed federalism to soften harsher predestinarianism, he suggests that this is not so in the case of Owen, 'since Owen uses covenant theology both in his Commentary as well as in his *The Doctrine of Justification by Faith* (1677) in order to emphasise the sovereignty and predestination of God'.[54] But this is to beg the question of harshness. Is it not possible to adopt the federal position with a view to emphasising the sovereignty and predestination of God and yet to avoid harshness? This, we suggest, is what Owen attempted, and we concur with G. P. Fisher who, long before Dr. Miller, expressed the view that 'The scheme of the Covenants, whatever may be thought of it in other respects, softened the rigor of Calvinistic teaching by setting up jural relations in the room of bare sovereignty'.[55] In similar vein W. Adams Brown wrote:

'Artificial in its account of the relation between God and man, it [i.e. the covenant theology] was in reality designed as a protest against arbitrariness . . . To its more earnest advocates the covenant theology, as distinct from the type of thought which it opposed, expressed the difference between a God whose purpose was known and whose character could be trusted, and a God whose nature was mysterious and whose actions were unpredictable. Few terms were richer in experimental significance to those who had been trained to understand it . . . "The covenant", says Edward Leigh, in the title to his *Treatise of the Divine Promises,* Lond. 1633, "is itself the bundle and body of all the promises".'[56]

The quotation from Leigh reminds us that, contrary to the opinion of some of their opponents of their own and later times, the seventeenth century Calvinists were not all cold, unimpassioned, 'cerebral' men. Rutherford could write in the tenderest terms (not least from prison) of the presence and solace of Christ.[57] A lesser known Calvinist, John Mason (1646?–1694) could plead with sinners in the most winsome of tones:

> 'Have you sins, or have you none? If you have, whither should you go, but to the Lamb of God, which taketh away the sins of the world? . . . Come as you are; come poor, come needy, come naked, come empty, come wretched, only come, only believe; His heart is free, His arms are open; 'tis His joy and His crown to receive you. If you are willing, He never was otherwise.'[58]

John Owen himself, for all his ability to *write* drily, was of the company of the 'twice-born' and had a genuine experimental knowledge of the grace of which he wrote.[59] It was this which undergirded his Calvinism, and made him determined to wage war upon Arminianism and all its works. In 1643 there appeared his *Display of Arminianism, Being a Discovery of the old Pelagian Idol, Free will, etc.,* in which he strongly urged predestinarian doctrine against the increasingly fashionable Laudian Arminianism. In the wake of Calvin himself Owen upheld man's free agency: for him, man was no automaton. In later works Owen defended such crucial doctrines as the limited atonement and the perseverance of the saints. As an illustration of his method, and as representing the heart of his position, we may quote his own words in which he faces the Arminians with the consequences of their position respecting the atonement:

> 'A spreading persuasion there is of *a general ransom* to be paid by Christ for all; that he died to redeem *all and every one* . . . Now, the masters of this opinion do see full well and easily, that if *that* be the *end* of the death of Christ which we have from the Scripture asserted [i.e. that Christ died for the *elect* only] . . . then one of these two things will necessarily follow: that either, first, God and Christ failed of their end proposed . . . which to assert seems to us blasphemously injurious to the wisdom, power, and

perfection of God, as likewise derogatory to the worth and value of the death of Christ; — or else, that all men . . . must be saved, purged, sanctified, and glorified; which surely they will not maintain, at least the Scripture and the woeful experience of millions will not allow. Wherefore, to cast a tolerable colour upon their persuasion, they must and do deny that God or his Son had any such absolute aim or end in the death or blood-shedding of Jesus Christ . . . but that God intended nothing, neither was anything effected by Christ, — that no benefit ariseth to any immediately by his death but what is common to all and every soul . . .'[60]

Such is the position which Owen sets out to refute in the interests of sovereign grace.

We turn now to the antinomian controversy which was productive of much heat and some light, and which found Baxter, Rutherford and Owen and others standing foursquare against the common foe. Not indeed that they were averse to taking one another to task when occasion demanded — as when Baxter accused Owen of antinomianism in his *The Death of Death*.[61] The antinomian tendency may be traced right back to the New Testament, where we find Paul making the classical orthodox response to it. Some have accused him of teaching that evil must be done that good may come. He denies this, and insists that far from faith's being the means of undermining the law, 'we are placing law itself on a firmer footing'.[62] The Valentinian gnostics, by virtue of their dualism of the divine energy (πνεῦμα) and the soul/body (ψῡχή), countenanced the licentiousness of the latter, deeming the former to be in no danger therefrom. Again, some Anabaptists taught and practised antinomianism. They were, they held, under grace, and consequently the law had no rights over them. With Johann Agricola (c. 1494—1566) the antinomian debate of Reformation times came to a head. It was his intention to underline the impossibility of a righteousness achieved by works, and as J. MacBride Sterrett points out, he considered that his exposition was quite in line with that of Luther, who had branded the letter of James 'an epistle of straw' because of its advocacy of good works, and who had criticised those who would so have emphasised

legalism as to 'make Jews of us through Moses'. Nor did
Agricola doubt that Melanchthon would support him, for the
latter had declared that 'It must be admitted that the
Decalogue is abrogated'.[63] So it was that at Wittenberg in
1537 Agricola maintained the indifference of works in a public disputation, and said, 'Art thou steeped in sin, an adulterer,
or a thief? If thou believest, thou art in salvation. All who
follow Moses must go to the devil. To the gallows with
Moses'.[64] This was too much for Luther, and he gave to the
heresy the name by which it is known today. Calvin likewise
refers to 'certain ignorant persons' who 'rashly cast out the
whole of Moses, and bid farewell to the two Tables of the
Law . . . [In fact] Moses has admirably taught that the law,
which among sinners can engender nothing but death, ought
among the saints to have a better and more excellent use . . .
the law is not now acting towards us as a rigorous enforcement officer who is not satisfied unless the requirements are
met. But in this perfection to which it exhorts us, the law
points out the goal toward which throughout life we are to
strive'.[65]

The American antinomian controversy of the seventeenth
century flared up around the determined and provocative
Mrs. Ann Hutchinson (1591–1643), who was supported by
her brother-in-law John Wheelwright, and opposed by
Governor John Winthrop (1588–1649). Into the details of
the case we need not go.[66] Suffice it to say that in Winthrop's
own words of 21st October 1636, Mrs. Hutchinson,

> 'a member of the church of Boston, a woman of a ready
> wit and bold spirit, brought over with her two dangerous
> errors: (1) That the person of the Holy Ghost dwells in a
> justified person. (2) That no sanctification can help to
> evidence to us our justification. From these two grew
> many branches; as: our union with the Holy Ghost, so as a
> Christian remains dead to every spiritual action, and hath
> no gifts nor graces, other than such as are in hypocrites,
> nor any other sanctification but the Holy Ghost himself.'[67]

Mrs. Hutchinson claimed that her views were in harmony with
those of John Cotton (1584–1652), teacher in the Boston
congregation, and that the remainder of the New England

clergy — not excluding John Wilson, pastor of the Boston church, were preaching a legalism which took no account of the activity of the Holy Spirit. She, on the other hand, taught that the believer is *immediately* possessed by the Spirit; that neither works preparatory to, nor consequent upon conversion are of any avail; and, for good measure, she had had revelations to prove it. Since the elders maintained that spiritual revelations of the kind claimed ceased with the apostles, they concluded that Satan had overtaken Mrs. Hutchinson, and they banished her to Rhode Island. In 1642 she moved to New Rochelle, where she was murdered by Indians — 'the news of her death being greeted in Massachusetts Bay as a divine confirmation of the community's sentence upon her'.[68]

Since, as John Winthrop wrote in 1637, 'it began to be as common here to distinguish between men, by being under a covenant of grace or a covenant of works, as in other countries between Protestants and Papists . . .'[69] John Cotton was required to make his position clear. He was pressed to preach against antinomianism, which he did; but at the Synod of October 1636, after much ministerial discussion, an inconclusive position was reached. As the trial of Mrs. Hutchinson proceeded Cotton clarified his position, and in particular he affirmed his view that while the Christian may properly derive assurance from the evidence of the Spirit's working in his life, he would revert to a covenant of works (and also, we would add, be beguiled into an unduly introspective attitude which would turn his gaze inward upon himself and away from Christ — as happened, for example, in some nineteenth-century Gadsbyite circles) if he believed that his justification was caused by, and was directly attributable to, his performance of such works.

But the essential divide between Cotton and Mrs. Hutchinson, and the elders, was not over the question of the place of works; neither side entertained a doctrine of salvation by works. What really upset the elders was the view which asserted the ontological union of the believer with the Holy Spirit at the moment of conversion. We mistake the nature of the controversy if we suppose that Cotton and Mrs. Hutchinson were maintaining Calvinism against Arminianism (the latter represented by the elders). The crux of the matter, as W. K. B. Stoever makes plain, was that the elders considered that *they* were maintaining the genuine Reformed position, according to which, to use Kierkegaard's term, there is an 'infinite qualitative difference' between God and men; and that God employs such means as the Word and the sacraments, together with infused habits, in the effecting of his foreordained purposes. Thus Stoever quotes John Norton (1606–63) as follows:

> 'We on the one hand against the Enthusiasts affirm not only the power to use, but the duty of using the means; and on the other hand, against the Arminians deny that man before grace can do anything, having the power of a cause (so far forth as comes from them) in order to life; because we are reasonable creatures God proceeds with us in the use of means; because we are dead creatures, in respect of the efficacy of the means, we depend wholly and absolutely upon God.'[70]

In contrast, Cotton and Ann Hutchinson came to hold that the believer can literally do nothing; that his works are not his own, but Christ's — with all that this entailed concerning the reduction of man's proper humanity. In short, they lost the first two words of the antinomy, 'I, yet not I, but Christ'. We may thus agree with Dr. Jones that the antinomian controversy, with its exaltation of God's sovereignty at the expense of man's responsibility, led to the shattering of the Calvinist synthesis of faith and works. On one side of the parted ways we find Calvinism represented notably by Jonathan Edwards (1703–58), and on the other side we find Arminianism-tending-to-unitarianism represented by Charles Chauncy (1705–87). Dr. Stoever seems to have right on his side in concluding that the elders were trying to maintain the synthesis which Cotton and Mrs. Hutchinson between them were violating. Indeed, we might *almost* say of both American and English antinomianism, that we have a Christian family dispute of the most intimate kind — it takes place under the Calvinist roof. We qualify the remark in deference to Dr. Nuttall, who reminds us that

'Calvinism's opposite, whether Arminianism, universalism or

enthusiasm, can also degenerate into antinomianism, though of a more practical kind. Here an emphasis on the uncondi-tioned love of God for all men, or on the ability of men, by their reason or their innate goodness, to have some share in their salvation, at least by way of response to God's grace, can breed a tolerant compassionateness, and then a loose permissiveness, wholly antipathetic to the fulfilment of law divine or human.'[71]

Dr. Nuttall's words provide the occasion for entering an important caveat before we view the English scene once more. It is necessary when considering antinomianism to bear in mind the distinction between its doctrinal and its practical varieties. The vast majority of those who tended towards antinomianism occupy the former class. Thus, none of those to whom we have referred or shall refer were libertines. Per-haps, in the interests of consistency, some of them *ought* to have been, as Locke held;[72] but most men are, happily, better than their worst beliefs. It is, in fact, most difficult to find instances of practical antinomianism, partly because records of ecclesiastical discipline are few and far between. A fairly well documented case is that of David Crosley (1670—1744) of Bacup who had, it appears, a predilection for antinomianism alcohol, and female company — these last two sufficing to cause his excommunication from his charge at the Currier's Hall to which he had gone in 1705, and which he left in disgrace in 1709.[73] We should like to know on what basis W. T. Whitley said that 'the antinomianism of *many* caused frequent scandals',[74] and we could wish that Dr. Elliott-Binns had distinguished between doctrinal and practical antinomianism when he argued that Robert Hall's attacks on this doctrine evidenced the extent and influence of the tendency.[75] All the same, we cannot deny the validity of James Buchanan's judgment:

'It becomes us to remember, that the Antinomian Theory is one thing, and the Antinomian Tendency another, — that the one may be comparatively rare, while the other is alike natural and inveterate, — and that the danger of practical, if not of speculative, Antinomianism, must always exist, as long as the doctrines of Grace are presented to the minds which are either entirely carnal, or as yet imperfectly sanctified . . . and the last day only will declare how much practical Antinomianism has prevailed even in Evangelical congregations, which theoretically disowned it . . .'[76]

One further cautionary word is necessary before we briefly review English antinomianism. We must at all times be aware of the zeal with which, in those earnest, pamphleteering days, writers would resort to abuse by nick-name. We must not, therefore, assume that a writer is an antinomian until we have examined his writings, for in some cases the term is one of abuse.[77] More frequently, perhaps, some authors, by reason of ambiguous expression, leave themselves open to more than one interpretation. Of few is this as true as it is of Tobias Crisp (1600–43),[78] regarded by some, then as now, as the high priest of English antinomianism. Thus, a recent writer, Roger Thomas, categorically asserts that Crisp was 'a notorious Antinomian';[79] Dr. James I. Packer admits that 'in the view of some' Crisp was antinomian, but, somewhat uncharacteristically, leaves us unsure of his own opinion;[80] and Crisp's *D.N.B.* biographer properly notes that (as all would agree) 'his writings certainly do not show that he had any intention of defending licentiousness'.[81] This is, in fact, to put it mildly, for Crisp lambasted the licentious as being 'the greatest enemies of the free grace of God, the greatest subverters of the power and purity of the gospel . . .'[82] Our own view is that Crisp is ambiguous; that it was genuinely his intention to ascribe salvation solely to God's grace; but that, partly out of a desire to avoid a wrong emphasis upon works, he over-played his hand in resisting the believer's desire to verify his assurance from those spiritual graces which the Spirit imparted to him. This was the burden of Rutherford's complaint, which is presented in his anti-antinomian tract, *A Survey of the Spiritual Anti-Christ* (1648), and which finds its way into his other writings too:

'If we cannot gather any assurance of our spiritual estate, from holy duties in us, such as are universal obedience, sincerity in keeping close to Christ, and love to the saints, because they may deceive us, and may be in hypocrites, as

Doctor Crispe saith, then may faith also deceive us; for there be as many kinds of false faiths, as there be of counterfeit loves to the saints; and there is somewhat of Christ peculiar to the regenerate in their love, obedience, and sincerity, which they may discern to be a saving character, and badge of Christ, no less than in faith.'[83]

We should not conclude, however, that Crisp had no place at all for works. The general tenor of his writings, and especially of his sermons XLV—XLVIII is that free grace, though not earned by good works, should inspire such works. Again, in answer to the question, 'But must not we serve in duty, will you say?' he replies, 'ye must serve in duty and obedience, but look not that that duty should bring any thing; it is Christ brings every thing you get . . . So far as Christ is slighted, and other things promoted above him, so far you take away the great end for which Christ was sent into the world, which was, "That he might have the pre-eminence in all things".'[84]

Rutherford further attacked Crisp's view that men are justified from eternity — a position which had earlier been maintained by Twisse, and which was countered by the Westminster divines in the following terms: 'God did, from all eternity, decree to justify all the elect; and Christ did, in the fulness of time, die for their sins, and rise again for their justification; nevertheless they are not justified, until the Holy Spirit doth in due time actually apply Christ unto them.'[85] But perhaps Crisp never sailed so near the wind as when he taught that Christ actually *becomes* sin. This view, which imperils the orthodox understanding of justification and imputation, is elaborated in sermon XVIII on *Isaiah 53:6*. Even here, though, Crisp seeks to guard his flank, and *intends* — for all his ambiguous phraseology — to stress only the *fact* of Christ *qua* sin-bearer:

'Indeed, let us not make God so childish: if he laid iniquity on Christ, he past this real act upon him, and the thing is thus really, as he disposes of it; and therefore, in brief, this laying iniquity upon him, is such a translation of sin from those whose iniquity he lays upon him, that by it he now becomes, or did become, when they were laid, as really and truly the person that had all these sins, as those men who did commit them really and truly had them themselves: it is true, as I said before, Christ never sinned in all his life; "He did no violence, neither was any deceit in his mouth"; but this hinders not, but that there may be on him an absolute transaction; so that by laying iniquity on him, he becomes the sole person in the behalf of all the elect, that truly hath iniquity upon him.'[86]

Certainly there was a tendency in Crisp's thought in the direction of telescoping regeneration, justification, and sanctification to such a degree that the believer's obligation to work out his own salvation was ruled out of court. Some of Crisp's contemporaries, John Eaton (1575—1641) for example, went further in this direction than he did.[87] But we should remember the force of the Arminian threat to such men as Crisp. Indeed, in his earlier days he had been of that persuasion himself — and converts seldom move a *little* way from their formerly held position. With an eye to the debate within Calvinism which was subsequently to develop over the question of evangelism and the 'offer' of the gospel, we may fittingly conclude our account of Crisp with one of his characteristically winsome appeals:

'Doth Satan seek to overcome you by his temptations, and, like a roaring lion, to devour you? He is able to tread down Satan under your feet. Beloved, will you starve in a cook's shop, as they say? Is there such plenty in Christ, and will you perish for hunger? You will answer, it may be, you would close with him, you would go to him for supply with all your hearts, but you dare not, you are afraid he will reject you, if you come to him. Beloved, come to Christ, and he will not cast you off.'[88]

One writer chillingly introduces the next phase of the English antinomian debate with the sub-title, 'Enter Tobias Crisp's Ghost':[89] and the more devious-minded may consider this peculiarly appropriate, since it was an undertaker by the name of Marshall who encouraged Samuel Crisp to republish his father's works in 1689—90. Apart from the fact of republication itself, there were two features of the venture which angered Richard Baxter. Firstly, his views were attacked in the preface; and secondly, twelve ministers signed a certificate authenticating eight sermons which had not been included in the editions of 1643 and 1646. Among these ministers was John Howe (1630–1705),[90] whom Baxter knew to be opposed to Crisp's teaching, and who afterwards confessed that he had read neither the sermons nor the preface. By way of recompense Howe published a denial of sympathy with Crispianism and, together with six of the original twelve signatories, he included a further disclaimer in a supplement to John Flavel's Πλανηλογια *A succinct and seasonable discourse* . . . (1691). The revival of Crispianism rubbed salt in the wound which Baxter had sustained when, in 1687 the Independent Thomas Cole (1627?–1697)[91] replaced John Collins on the panel of Merchant's Lecturers. In 1688 Cole delivered his lecture, published later under the title, *A Discourse of Regeneration* (1689), in which he took that High Calvinistic line which consorted ill with Baxter's more moderate Amyraldism. Cole shortly followed this up with *The Incomprehensibleness of Imputed Righteousness for Justification by Human Reason, till enlightened by the Spirit of God* (1692) — a title which adequately summarises his main point. By now Samuel Crisp had entered the lists in his own right. In 1691 there appeared his *Christ made sin evidenced from Scripture,* and this was followed by a number of further, heated defenses of his father's views. The saddest practical result of this controversy was the sundering of that Happy Union between Presbyterians and Independents which Baxter had worked so hard to achieve.

Few during this period trod the middle ground between antinomianism and Baxterism more graciously than the Presbyterian Thomas Watson and the Independent Samuel Young. Thus, for example, Watson summed up the place of the moral law as follows:

'In some sense it is abolished to believers. (1) In respect of justification. They are not justified by their obedience to the moral law, but they must trust only to Christ's righteousness for justification . . . If the moral law could justify, what need was there of Christ's dying? (2) The moral law is abolished to believers, in respect of its curse.'[92]

Again, Young argued, in his *An Apology for Congregational Divines* (1698), that 'High Calvinism' and 'antinomianism' are not synonymous terms, and that it is possible to subscribe to the former and to shun the latter. All of which was a reaffirmation of the position reached many years before by the Westminster and Savoy divines.

The somewhat rougher diamond Richard Davis (1658–1714), did not manage to strike a happy medium.[93] Of the Independent persuasion, he had been a member of Thomas Cole's congregation, and, on 22nd March 1690 he was ordained at Rothwell. In refusing to invite neighbouring ministers to his ordination service he flouted the ecumenical conventions of the time, and by his proselytising zeal he rode rough-shod over the finer points of clerical manners. As if this were not enough, he preached doctrinal antinomianism. He absented himself from an assembly of ministers appointed to consider his views, branding the event the 'Kettering Inquisition'. Daniel Williams (1643?–1715), a Presbyterian and Baxterian, was appointed to refute his teaching. Williams's book, *The Gospel Truth Stated* (1692), on which he had been working since the revival of Crispianism, reinforced the position of those who sided with him. Antinomianism was not the only question at issue. Some Independents, led by Isaac Chauncy, were irritated by such Presbyterian predilections as synodical trial and censure; and were also as hostile towards antinomianism as they were to the Arminianism and Socinianism which they were quite sure they detected in Williams. 'With as much justice they might have accused him of being a worshipper of the Delai Lama of Tartary', opined Bogue and Bennett.[94] Chauncy stated his position in *Neonomianism Unmasked* (in three parts 1692–3); Williams promptly replied, and in 1693 Chauncy published a *Rejoynder* to him. Meanwhile, in 1692 P. Rehakosht (i.e. John King) sent forth his *A Plain and just account of a most horrid and dismal plague begun at Rowell, alias Rothwell, in Northamptonshire.* This was an attack both upon Davis's churchly indelicacies and upon his antinomianism. In his reply, *Truth and Innocency Vindicated* (1692) Davis showed no great desire either to deny his 'sins' or to repent of them. In 1693 Giles Firmin published *A Brief Review of Mr. Davis's Vindication;* and there the matter rested. The judgment of Bogue and Bennett on the entire Crispian affair displays the horror with which later Calvinists viewed the episode:

'Dr. Crisp was one of the first patrons of Calvinism run
mad, which has of late polluted and tormented the
churches . . . Glorying in the name of Calvin, whose works
they never read, or they would have branded him with the
epithet of an Arminian, these zealots proclaimed the
sovereignty of God, not in the spirit of Jesus or his apostles,
with humble awful adoration, but with the temper of
fiends who wished to render it odious and repulsive . . .
Eternal justification and sancitifaction were made to super-
cede repentance for sin, and pursuit of holiness; the very
word duty was abhorred; the law of God vilified; and, while
the most ridiculously allegorical interpretations of Scripture
were applauded as proofs of inspiration, all addresses to
sinners were anathematised as rank arminianism . . . It
should . . . be noted that this poison has been swallowed by
evangelical churchmen, and even by some of the clergy, as
well as by dissenters.'[95]

Our historians could have obviated the difficulties: 'Had the
good men been properly cooled by a "fine mild act", or
immured in prison for half a year . . . they would have found
out, that there was neither arminianism nor antinomianism to
be renounced; but the ignorance of some to be removed, the
bigotry of others to be cured, and many bad tempers to be
mortified and subdued.'[96] All they could do was to express
this hope: 'May the beacon, which the writers in this controversy erected, be seen, and the dangerous quicksands avoided
by all their successors from age to age.'[97]

It is sometimes alleged that, partly because of 'cramping'
Calvinism, the seventeenth century saw little of missionary
zeal or evangelistic fervour. There are, however, some
witnesses to the contrary. Richard Baxter, for example, who
enthusiastically corresponded with John Eliot (1604–90) the
apostle to the American Indians, was a keen supporter of the
movement which led to the formation of the Society for the
Propagation of the Gospel (1701); and such a High Calvinist
as Richard Davis could not be confined within one building.
Others, for the most solemn of reasons, took a different
view, and among these Joseph Hussey (1659–1726)[98] was
prominent. He had been ordained a Presbyterian and, moreover, one of the kind opposed to High Calvinism. In this

capacity he had attacked the position of Davis at the 'Kettering Inquisition'. From 1694, however, his church at Cambridge 'openly practised the Congregational order'.[99] With this change of churchmanship there went a change of doctrine, and Hussey became a High Calvinist — indeed, he surpassed his erstwhile opponent Davis in the rigour of his views. Not only did he now hold to particular redemption, he became unusually circumspect in the terms he employed in preaching. He was especially concerned that to speak of 'offering' the gospel might imply an innate ability on the part of unaided fallen man to accept the gospel. He expressed his concern at length in his *God's Operations of Grace but no Offers of Grace* (1707). The following summary will make his position plain, and will also clarify the position against which Andrew Fuller's more moderate Calvinism was later to be pitted:

> 'By offers of grace, tenders and proffers of salvation, it is evident, men do thereby imply that free grace and full salvation is propounded, tendered, and offered to all sinners within the sound . . . Is not this a piece of robbery against the Holy Spirit? . . . Does not the plea confine the operations of the Holy Spirit to common and eternal workings? Wherein does your plea give Jehovah the Spirit His due honour in the internal and mighty workings of His grace on sinner's hearts, that sinners may believe, repent, and be saved?'[100]

Hussey proceeds to distinguish between offering Christ to sinners, and preaching Christ to sinners. 'By preaching, the doctrine of the Gospel is carried home to the hearers, whether they will or no . . . Offers are bringing the things and leaving them at a distance over against them, which wait for acceptance before the things proposed or offered can approach unto them, or be approached unto . . . Preaching the Gospel, is a revealing act . . . [it] has to do with the elect of God . . . Offers rob the Father, and rob Christ, and the Holy Spirit, and the soul and all.'[101] A very serious objection to offers is that they undermine the necessity of imputation: 'The Spirit will not, and cannot honourably work without the imputation of Christ; but offers of Christ are without a due regard of the imputation of his righteousness, or the work of the Spirit, therefore are not fit means to work this ability. [i.e. the ability to close with Christ].'[102] There is thus all the difference in the world between the offer of grace, and God's *gift* of grace. Hussey then asks what becomes of preaching if his approach is adopted. Does it follow that preaching is of no avail? No, for although the elect alone will receive God's gift of grace, the preacher does not know who they are, and must therefore preach Christ to all and sundry: 'The Lord enable all his ministers to preach discreetly; and while they preach the Gospel, not to propound it as an offer, but preach the Gospel doctrine to all, and preach the salvation of the Gospel with their hearts salvation-wise, towards the elect of God alone. Finally, the Lord grant, that we may neither attempt to rob the Father's gift, nor the Spirit's power, by degrading God's faithfulness into man's flattery. Amen, Amen.'[103]

Hussey then applies his doctrine in a number of ways, one of which is of particular interest to us. He regards his position as securing the gospel against Arminian erosion. Whereas 'We are ready to think Arminianism lies only in prayer-books, altars, and Roman-Catholic churches; and that if we protest against the Canons of the Synod of Dort, all is well. This is another mistake. Arminianism is the universal nature of mankind . . . I find it as natural in me to be an Arminian, as it is to breathe . . . We were all born so, and without the power of grace we must die so . . . Arminius, too near akin to Pelagius, makes use of the offer to uphold the doctrine of general redemption . . .'[104] Moreover, 'Offers of Christ to unregenerate sinners are suited to creature-co-operation, and creature-concurrence, which is rank Arminianism'.[105] As Principal Macleod said of this variety of High Calvinism, 'when we look into it, we find the common Arminian position that man's responsibility is limited by his ability. The Arminian holds to the presence of a certain ability in those that are called; otherwise sinners could not be called upon to repent and believe the Gospel. Each side takes up the principle from its own end. They fail together to recognise that the sinner is responsible for his spiritual impotence'.[106]

The effects of the stance which Hussey typifies were felt especially keenly amongst the English Particular Baptists, as we shall shortly see. There were many, however, who wished both to resist Arminianism, and to proclaim the gospel more experimentally and generously than the stricter Calvinism seemed to permit. To this class belonged Scotland's Marrowmen.[107] The *Marrow of Modern Divinity* was published in 1646 by one 'E.F.', over whose identity controversy has raged.[108] A collection of generally received High Calvinist teachings, it provoked little comment at the time. One who claimed to have been more influenced by it than by any other book was James Fraser of Brea (1639–99),[109] the Covenanter who, when a prisoner on the Bass Rock wrote his *Justifying Faith,* which remained unpublished during his life-time — and, indeed, may never have been intended for publication. When it did appear in 1749 it caused a stir, and drew the fire of Adam Gib. The charge was that Fraser taught universal redemption, and although a recent writer considers that Fraser did in fact advance the cause of universalism in Scotland,[110] Fraser himself disclaimed any intention of teaching universalism of an Arminian kind, though he did feel constricted by the kind of approach represented by Hussey. What in fact he held came to be known as the double reference theory of the atonement, according to which 'Christ obeyed, and died in the room of all, as the head representative of fallen man'. Notwithstanding this, God intended to save only the elect. The purpose of Christ's death is principally to glorify God, and that both in saving and damning. Satisfaction having been rendered for all, and the gospel offered to all, God is glorified both by the response of the saved and the response of the damned, which latter class come not under law, but under *gospel* wrath. What Macleod calls 'this bizarre doctrine of a redemption that issues and was meant to issue in nothing else than greater wrath for the lost'[111] is the result of Fraser's attempt to avoid the dilemma of either not offering the gospel, or else implying man's ability to accept it — and both to the hurt of God's glory. The outcome was, however, that the justice of God was impugned. Not surprisingly, later universalists were most selective in their use, if any, of Fraser; but of his evangelistic intentions there can be no question.

The story of Thomas Boston's discovery in 1700 of two books in the home of one of his parishioners at Simprin has often been told.[112] One book, by Saltmarsh, did not appeal to him; but the second, *The Marrow,* moved him greatly. In the first part of it Evangelista, a true minister of the gospel, demolishes the arguments of Nomista the legalist, and Antinomista, the antinomian. In the second part Evangelista expounds the decalogue, pithily expressing the orthodox reformed position on the law of works and the law of Christ thus: 'Both these laws agree in saying, Do this. But here is the difference. The one saith, Do this and live; and the other saith, Live and do this. The one saith Do this for life; the other saith Do this from life.'[113] It is not surprising that James Hervey (1714–58), the English Calvinistic methodist could describe *The Marrow* as 'a book designed to guard equally against Antinomian licentiousness and legal bondage'.[114] But the Scottish Church had meanwhile judged differently.

The occasion of the controversy was the so-called 'Auchterarder Creed'. As a bulwark against Arminianism the presbytery of Auchterarder composed the following affirmation to be confessed by candidates for license: 'I believe that it is not sound and orthodox to teach that we must forsake sin in order to our coming to Christ, and instating us in covenant with God.' This was, of course, a clumsily worded attempt to exclude works-righteousness, but it was open to an antinomian interpretation. One candidate refused to subscribe, was not licensed, and appealed to the General Assembly of 1717. The Assembly repudiated the presbytery's statement, reversed its (strictly improper) action, and authorised the licensing of the candidate in question. Boston was among those who attacked the Assembly's action, and in conversation with John Drummond of Crieff, he testified to the aid *The Marrow* had given him years earlier on the disputed issue. Drummond mentioned the matter to James Webster of Edinburgh, and he to James Hog of Carnock (1658?–1734), at whose behest the book was republished in 1718. The ensuing controversy was debated at the Assembly of 1720, Principal James Hadow (1670?–1747) being a leading opponent of *The Marrow.*[115] He favoured the High Calvinist position, but on this occasion he was joined by the more moderate Baxterian types. As Macleod says of Hadow, 'He laid his lance in rest and had a bout of tilting at windmills'.[116] He found what he took to be a number of antinomian statements in *The Marrow,* including one to the effect that the believer is not subject to the divine law as a rule of life, and another which suggested that holy living was not essential to salvation. The book was further criticised by the High Calvinists for teaching that Christ had effected a universal atonement. In this connection the Assembly took exception to the phrase which asserted that Christ's death was 'the deed of gift and grant to mankind lost'. Of course Boston and the Marrowmen (as they came to be called) were ardent defenders of particular redemption. They merely wished to urge that the warrant to believe is common to all, and that the believer may derive assurance from the evidence of the Spirit's working in him: 'Say then, I beseech you, with a firm faith, the righteousness of Jesus Christ belongs to all that believe; but I believe; and therefore it belongs to me'.[117]

Undeterred, the Assembly condemned the book. Subsequently Boston and eleven others, including Ebenezer and Ralph Erskine, presented a representation against the Assembly's Act, but on 28th May 1722 the Assembly reiterated its earlier decision, albeit in slightly modified form.[118]

In his able summing-up of the matter J. Macleod grants that to focus too much on personal feelings of assurance may, *especially when faith is weak,* obscure the fact that 'Christ is mine' in the offer of the gospel. For all that, the Marrow view 'was a persuasion or assurance that in the overtures of the Gospel the Saviour is held out to all to be by them taken as their own'.[119] In this it compared favourably with one of the opposing views, according to which introspection was encouraged in order to ascertain whether or not I am of the elect and therefore competent to receive the gospel. Walker duly appreciated the importance of the Marrowmen for the church's mission: 'Boston and the Marrow men, first of all among our divines, entered fully into the missionary spirit of the Bible; were able to see that Calvinistic doctrine was not inconsistent with world-conquering aspirations and efforts.'[120] Wales was on the point of learning the same lesson.

CHAPTER THREE

In Full Spate

In 1713 Matthias Maurice (1684–1738)[1] came from Wales to be pastor at Olney, Buckinghamshire; in 1723 he succeeded Davis at Rothwell. He left a trail of secession behind him in his native land, and yet again the disputed issue seems to have been that of High Calvinism and its concomitant antinomian peril. (That Maurice subsequently radically changed his views we shall shortly see). Dr. Nuttall recounts that in 1691 the moderate, Presbyterian members of the dissenting church in Wrexham left their High Calvinist Congregational brethren and formed the New Meeting. Among their supporters was James Owen, whose brother, D. J. Owen, was pastor at Henllan, Carmarthenshire from 1705–10. During his pastorate Maurice, a member of the Henllan church, led the High Calvinists out to form a new cause, of Congregationalist persuasion, at Rhyd-y-ceisiaid. When, in 1711, Maurice 'poached' from the flock of Jeremy Owen, D.J.'s son and successor, he was reprimanded by the United Brethren (Presbyterian and Congregational) of Devon and Cornwall, and accused by Jeremy Owen of being a Crispite and a Davisite.[2] That Wales did not suffer a drastic and widespread polarisation of antinomian-Arminian views is owing to the emergence of that missionary-minded brand of Calvinism, one of whose founders, Daniel Rowland (1713–90) was born in the year of Maurice's departure for England. His co-worker, Howel Harris, was born in the following year and died in 1773.[3]

It appears that like others before and since, Rowland, the Anglican incumbent of Llangeitho, Cardiganshire, began to preach before he had been granted an experimental grasp of the truths he uttered. Among those who influenced him was Griffith Jones of Llanddowror, whose circulating charity

schools did so much to foster literacy in Wales. From Jones
Rowland learned the necessity of solemnly proclaiming the
law, and this he began to do. But it was the dissenting
minister Philip Pugh who exhorted him to preach the gospel
and 'apply the balm that is in Gilead'. When Rowland protested his lack of an existential grasp of the gospel, Pugh
replied (with a happy innocence of latter-day charges of auto-
suggestion!) 'preach it until you feel it. It will come without
fail. If you go on preaching the law after this fashion, you
will kill half the population . . .'[4] Rowland finally underwent
his conversion experience at about the same time that Howel
Harris of Talgarth enjoyed his — in 1735.

Harris's progress towards a fully Calvinistic position was
gradual. He himself informs us that 'in 1737, I was first
enlightened to see the Doctrine of Free Grace: although my
experience had shown me from the beginning that I could do
nothing in my own power'.[5] The puritan Thomas Shephard's
book, *The Sincere Convert* (1641) was of special help to him
at this time — it 'was used to turn me from duties and frames,
to depend only on Christ'. He proceeds to explain that for a
while he 'fell into believing in Reprobation', but was delivered
therefrom by reading *I Timothy* 2:4; *II Peter* 2:9; and *Ezekiel*
33:11.[6] Dr. Evans provides us with a list of those by whom
Harris was influenced. In addition to Shephard we find (to
cite only those whom we have mentioned elsewhere) Baxter,
Owen, Calvin, Ussher, Jonathan Edwards, Elisha Coles, and
John Cotton. Whitefield and Wesley, to whom we have yet to
refer in detail, are also listed.[7]

Harris was much encouraged when Whitefield opened correspondence with him on 20th December 1738. In a reply dated
8th January 1739· we find an early example of Harris's
testimony to the riches of free grace: 'I hope we shall be
taught more and more to admire the wonderful goodness of
God in His acts of free grace; sure no person is under such
obligation to advance the glory of His free goodness and grace
as this poor prodigal.'[8] Among other influences upon Harris
was that of the Moravians. On 26th April 1739 he visited the
Fetter Lane Society, London, and this together with his
numerous contacts with John Cennick (who deserted
methodism for the Moravians in 1745) taught him lessons in

experimental religion and Christian community which he never forgot. His later community at Trevecca was inspired by the Moravian settlements, and his debt to the brethren was such that when in July 1740 Wesley separated from the Moravians over the question of Wesleyan perfectionism *versus* Moravian quietism; and when Rowland forsook the Moravians because he saw antinomianism as the only logical consequence of their anti-works teaching, Harris maintained relations throughout.

In June 1739 Harris met John and Charles Wesley for the first time. Since Wesley's *Arminian* reputation had preceded him, Harris was pleasantly surprised by the preaching he heard. Not long afterwards, however, Wesley excommunicated a predestinarian from his society and, against Whitefield's advice — and during the latter's absence in America — published, in August 1739, his sermon on *Free Grace.* During the ensuing months Harris did all he could to prevent a breach between Wesley and Whitefield. The two following extracts from his letters will demonstrate his peace-making attitude and also show how his theology was developing:

'Who can take off the Rebellion from our Wills, the Idols from our Affections, and the Veil from our Understandings, but that Power that spake Light from Darkness, at first . . .? And what can move him to do all this, but his own free, sovereign Will, Love, and Pleasure? And what can his End be but his Glory? . . . I receiv'd a Letter from Brother *Seward,* and Brother *Ch. Wesley,* whereby I find that some Misunderstanding have been among them so as to separate. O sure I fear our dear Master is not pleased with this! and his Kingdom will not be thus established. — Labour for Peace, my dear Brother. — Though our Brother J.W. is not yet enlightened to see God's electing Love, yet as I firmly believe he is one of the Elect, God will in his own Time shew that to him, which now to some wise End is yet hid from him . . . I hope to write to Brother Seward and Brother Wesley. In the mean Time labour to unite them in Affections till the Lord does in Judgment more fully.[9]

'I have been long waiting to see if Brother *John* and *Charles* should receive farther Light, or be silent, and not *oppose Election* and *Perseverance*; but finding no Hope thereof, I begin to be stagger'd about them what to do. I

plainly see that we preach two Gospels, one sets *all on God,*
the other *on Man*; the one *on God's Will,* the other on
Man's Will; the one on *God's chusing,* the other on *Man's
chusing*; the one on *God's Distinguishing Love, making one
to differ from another*; the other on *Man's being better than
another, and taking more pains, and being a better husband
of his Grace than another, more* passive *under the Hand of
the Spirit than the other;* and if both shou'd come to Heaven
they cou'd not harmonise in Praises . . .

'One Reason staggers me much about all *Universalists,*
when there is an Appeal made to their Experiences, if then
they will not come to see *Electing Love.* For whoever has
Distinguishing Love, has Light with that, to see that he has
a *particular Favour,* and so is under a *particular Obligation*
to glorify God, and willingly takes away all Occasion of
glorying or boasting but that. For it is a wide Difference
to be saved or to be lost, to be for ever with God, and for-
ever with the Devil. And it is a Matter of the highest
Moment, that *whoever* or *whatever* makes the Difference
should have the Glory of it; it being the Hinge on which
turns our Salvation . . . Christ saith, *All that the Father
hath given to me shall come to me . . .* But Man says, *God*
draweth all alike, but some resist him. But did not we all
resist him 'till he drew us irresistably, so that we could not
be unwilling . . . What I am contending for, is the Glory of
his *Sovereign, Free, Unchangeable Love* to his Elect . . .
Those that say that preaching this is preaching Licentiousness to Man, and will make him careless, shew that they
never tasted this Love . . . *We are free in* Wales *from the
hellish* Infection [i.e. antinomianism], *but some that are
tainted when they come to* Bristol.'[10]

Harris concludes his postscript to the second letter quoted
with this request: 'Pray that I may taste more the Grace of
every Truth, that I may not be found contending for Words,
but for Truths that I feel' — and this is experimental (not
coldly cerebral) Calvinism if ever we saw it.

Despite Harris's efforts, the breach between Wesley and
Whitefield occurred in March 1741. Since Wesley proclaimed a
version of free grace, and since Whitefield made it plain in a
letter to Wesley that he himself offered Christ to all (thereby

opening himself to the charge of inconsistency from the Arminian side, and of Arminianism and Pelagianism from the Calvinistic side), it is necessary precisely to specify the area of disagreement. This will entail a brief account of the background of the disputants. First, however, two points must be made plain. It should be remembered that a number of men, both Calvinists and Arminians, who remained true to the Established Church, were zealous in evangelism. They included William Grimshaw (1708—63), William Romaine (1714—95), John Berridge (1716—93), John Newton (1725—1807), Henry Venn (1725—97), and John William Fletcher of Madeley (1729—85).[11] We here concentrate upon Whitefield and Wesley because they adequately exemplify the doctrinal debate which primarily concerns us. Secondly, we do not overlook the fact that some who broadly *shared* Whitefield's theological stance (that is, they were not Calvinists of the Hussey type), could not easily bring themselves to support the revivalism of the times. They feared emotionalism; or they were unhappy about the employment of unlettered preachers; or they did not wish to upset the Anglicans, or to fall foul of the Toleration Act by supporting field preaching. Thus, for example, although it appears that Isaac Watts (1674—1748) supported the transatlantic revivalism associated with Jonathan Edwards (1703—58)[12] and the first Awakening of 1735, he was not so keen on revivalist manifestations nearer home. In 1743 he took Philip Doddridge (1702—51) to task for sharing in the services at Whitefield's Tabernacle in September 1743; and the Coward Trustees, the principal supporters of Doddridge's Northampton Academy, were equally concerned.[13] It is probable, however, that the underlying fear of both Watts and the trustees was that to support revival was tantamount to acquiescence in that variety of evangelical Arminianism which was so prominent a feature of the contemporary scene.

Humanly speaking it would have been very difficult for John and Charles Wesley not to have been Arminians. True, their forebears included such stalwart Calvinist-Puritan names as John White, the vice-chairman of the Westminster Assembly — their paternal grandmother's father, who suffered at the hands of Laud for denouncing Arminianism; Dr. Annesley, their maternal grandfather; and their paternal grandfather and great-grandfather, both of whom had been ejected from their Dorsetshire livings in 1662.[14] But Samuel Wesley, Rector of Epworth, and his wife Susanna,[15] had come by their own routes to Arminianism, and to the Established Church. They had settled in 'Arminian country' — John Smyth the General Baptist was from nearby Gainsborough, and Dutch settlers had brought their Arminianism to eastern England. Samuel and Susanna did not abate in their criticisms of the Calvinistic doctrines of election and reprobation. As Susanna wrote to John in 1725: 'The Doctrine of Predestination, as maintained by rigid Calvinists, is very shocking, and ought utterly to be abhorred; because it charges the most holy God with being the Author of Sin.'[16] Finally, as Dr. Nuttall has remarked, Wesley's words, 'The world is my parish' 'have a peculiarly eighteenth-century ring. They breathe the universalism of the eighteenth century in a far larger sense than the theological and could scarcely have been uttered in any earlier age. But they also breathe the missionary and evangelical concern which was Wesley's overmastering passion.'.[17]

There is ample evidence to show that from the time of his conversion in 1735, Whitefield's Calvinism began to take systematic shape: 'About this time God was pleased to enlighten my soul, and bring me into the knowledge of His free grace, and the necessity of being justified in His sight *by faith only.*'[18] Whitefield proceeds to mention the books which influenced him. These include Alleine's *Alarm,* Baxter's *Call to the Unconverted,* and Janeway's *Life.*[19] Again, in his journal entry for 29th September 1739 Whitefield, now *en route* to America, recorded his pleasure in reading some passages from *The Preacher* by Dr. John Edwards of Cambridge;[20] and when on 24th December 1740 he replied to Wesley's sermon on Free Grace, he extolled both John Edwards's *Veritas Redux* and Elisha Coles's work on God's sovereignty.[21] Quite as important as any of these works, however, was his corres-pondance with Ralph Erskine, the Scottish seceder from whom he had received a letter, before sailing for America, on 18th May 1739.[22] By Saturday 9th June he was 'much pleased and edified' by reading Erskine's *Sermons.*[23]

The Calvinistic convictions with which Whitefield went to America were strongly reinforced while he was there — and that especially by Jonathan Edwards, whose zeal in proclamation impressed him as greatly as Edwards's more abstruse philosophical speculations mystified him. As to the former, Whitefield had written to Wesley on 24th May 1740: 'I dread your coming over to America, because the work of God is carried on here (and that in a most glorious manner), by doctrines quite opposite to those you hold . . .'[24] Nor did Whitefield simply receive from America: he gave too. He returned to England to find himself in controversy with Wesley over the latter's Free Grace sermon and his own reply to it.[25]

Both Whitefield and Wesley wished to remain loyal to what the former designated 'the good old doctrine of the Church of England'.[26] Undeniably, however, Wesley interpreted the Articles through the eyes of an evangelical Arminian. George Eayrs characterised Wesleyan thought thus:

'With almost ceaseless iteration the preachers taught the doctrines of universal depravity, universal redemption, the witness of the Spirit to Christian assurance, the duty of testimony, and sanctification or Christian perfection. Charles Wesley's characteristic line —

let me commend my Saviour to you,

was upon their lips, and they proclaimed the five universals: that all men needed salvation; that all men might be saved; that all men might know themselves saved; that all should declare their salvation; and that all might perfect holiness in the fear of the Lord.'[27]

Confronted by such preaching Whitefield wrote from Aberdeen to Wesley (from whom he was now alienated) on 10th October 1741. He put his finger upon two crucial points of dispute and, incidentally, makes clear the mediatorial role of Howel Harris:

'This morning I received a letter from brother Harris, telling me how he had conversed with you and your dear brother. May God remove all obstacles that now prevent our union! Though I hold particular election, yet I offer Jesus freely to every individual soul. You may carry sanctification to what degrees you will, only I cannot agree

with you that the in-being of sin is to be destroyed in
this life.'[28]

Happily, harmonious relations at the personal level were
restored between the two men in 1742, and although they
never agreed over doctrine it is noteworthy that Wesley was
chosen, and agreed, to deliver the oration at Whitefield's
funeral. A further disruption occurred in the evangelical
ranks when in 1755 Wesley and James Hervey (1714–58)[29]
divided over theological matters. Hervey, who had been at
Oxford with Whitefield and the Wesleys, had published his
Theron and Aspasio (1755) in which he defended the doctrine
of imputed righteousness – 'imputed nonsense' as Wesley
called it. Some Calvinists objected to the antinomian tendency
of Hervey's thought, and Wesley attacked him in his *A
Preservative against Unsettled Notions in Religion* (1758).

Meanwhile in March 1742 a breach had occurred between
Harris and Rowland – much to Whitefield's dismay. It appears
that personalities were as much involved as theological
principles. Ostensibly the dispute was over assurance, Harris
maintaining that the believer could not be a true believer and
not know it experientially. Rowland held, with Whitefield,
that it was possible to be in Christ and not to know it. Other
difficulties ensued. Rowland became increasingly authori-
tarian, and Harris began to use such unguarded and unqualified
expressions as that God died upon the Cross. In view of the
strife between their leaders, it is small wonder that after
Whitefield had presided over the first Welsh Calvinistic
Methodist Conference on 5th January 1743, he was chosen at
the second Conference, on 6th April, to serve as President
whenever he was available.[30] Matters were not helped when,
in mid-1760 David Jones of Cardiganshire, Rowland's nephew,
together with Mr. Popkins of Swansea, began proclaiming
Sandemanianism and antinomianism. The celebrated hymn
writer William Williams, Pantycelyn (1717–91), and others
opposed them, and in the result 'Popkins withdrew from the
connexion, and Jones in a short time turned out a reprobate
character'.[31]

Whitefield died in 1770. In the August of 1769 Harris and
Rowland, after an eighteen-year period of estrangement, shared
in the first anniversary services of Trevecca College, under

the auspices of Lady Huntingdon, and alongside the Arminian President of the College, Fletcher of Madeley. Such tranquillity was short lived. In 1770 the next phase of the Calvinist controversy began. As long ago as 1743 Wesley had modified his position on unconditional election, irresistible grace, and final perseverance — this with a view to fostering his now restored relationship with Whitefield. The same doctrinal issues were discussed at the first Wesleyan Conference in 1744. Wesley's problem was to defend his own understanding of God's free grace without falling into the trap of antinomianism, to which, he was sure, Moravianism led. Some of his followers remained uneasy concerning his pro-Whitefield concessions — indeed, at the 1744 Conference Wesley himself declared that he had 'unawares leaned too much towards Calvinism';[32] though in the following year he granted that 'the true Gospel touches the very edge of Calvinism'. The antinomian threat never entirely subsided. In 1756 (the year after John Gill had republished Crisp's *Works*) Wesley detected signs of it among his own members in Manchester, and by 1770 he was dismayed to find that it had 'spread like wildfire' through his societies, and that those at Norwich, Manchester and Dublin had been particularly adversely affected.[33]

In March 1770 Wesley attacked the views of the ardent Anglican Calvinist Augustus Montague Toplady (1740—78),[34] whose (at this distance) engagingly vindictive language is almost as well known as his hymn 'Rock of ages'. Until his conversion to Calvinism in 1758 Toplady had been a supporter of Wesley, and in 1758 he had written a letter to Wesley in which he joined the latter in criticising some of Hervey's opinions. In 1769, however, he published *The Church of England Vindicated from the Charge of Arminianism*,[35] and when this was followed in 1769 by his *Life of Zanchy,* Wesley was provoked into writing his twelve-page rejoinder entitled, *The Doctrine of Absolute Predestination Stated and Asserted, by the Rev. A. T.* He here mercilessly parodied Toplady's views, concluding that 'The sum of all is this: one in twenty (suppose) of mankind are elected; nineteen in twenty are reprobated. The elect shall be saved, do what they will; the reprobate shall be damned, do what they can. Reader, believe

this, or be damned. Witness my hand, A- T-.'.[36] There followed
Toplady's *A Letter to Mr. Wesley* (1770), and Wesley's *The
Consequence Proved* (1771). Next came Toplady's full scale
work entitled *More Work for Mr. John Wesley* (1772). By now,
however, Wesley had left Toplady to the mercies of one of
his preachers, the former baker, Walter Sellon, who, though
earnest, was not the intellectual equal of Toplady.

The Wesleyan Conference had, meanwhile, discussed the
situation, and the following are extracts from the Minutes of
1770:

> 'We said, in 1744, "We have leaned too much toward
> Calvinism". Wherein?
>
> 1. With regard to *man's faithfulness* . . . We ought steadily
> to assert . . . that, if a man is not "faithful in the un-
> righteous mammon", God will not give *him the true riches.*
>
> 2. With regard to *working for life* . . . in fact, every
> believer, till he comes to glory, works for as well as *from*
> life.
>
> 3. We have received it as a maxim, that "a man is to do
> nothing in order to justification". Nothing can be more
> false. Whoever desires to find favour with God should
> "cease from evil, and learn to do well". Whoever repents
> should do "works meet for repentance". And if this is not
> *in order* to find favour, what does he do them for? . . .
> [Salvation is] Not by the *merit* of works, but by works as
> a *condition.* What have we been disputing about for these
> thirty years? I am afraid, *about words.* '[37]

Fletcher defended these minutes in his *Check to Antinomianism* (1771), a letter to Hon. the Reverend Walter
Shirley (1725–86),[38] a cousin of the Countess of Huntingdon.
Of this *Check,* and those that followed it[39] Wesley wrote, 'One
knows not which to admire most — the purity of the language
the strength and clearness of the argument, or the mildness
and sweetness of the spirit which breathes throughout the
whole'.[40] In making his own position clear to Fletcher
Wesley wrote, 'I always did, for between these thirty or forty
years, clearly assert the total fall of man and his utter
inability to do any good of himself; the absolute necessity of
the Grace and Spirit of God to raise even a good thought or

desire in our heart; the Lord's rewarding no work and accepting of none but so far as they proceed from the preventing, convincing, and converting grace through the Beloved; the blood and righteousness of Christ being the sole meritorious cause of our salvation. Who is there in England that has asserted these things more strongly and steadily than I have done?'.[41] The Countess was not appeased. Despite Wesley's admission that the minutes had been badly phrased, and Shirley's hesitant affirmation to the effect that he had misread them, a heated discussion broke out and, in a fit of temper, or as an act of prophetic symbolism (depending on one's point of view) the Countess consigned the 1770 *Minutes* to the flames. Joseph Benson, whom Wesley and Fletcher had nominated to be Headmaster at Trevecca, was forced to resign; and shortly Fletcher resigned from the post of President of the College. The 1776 Conference averred that

'Calvinism had been the grand hindrance to the work of God; and, hence, to stop its progress, all the preachers were requested — (1) To read with carefulness, the tracts published by Wesley, Fletcher and Sellon. (2) To preach universal redemption frequently, explicitly, and lovingly. (3) Not to imitate the Calvinist preachers in screaming, allegorising, and boasting; but to visit as diligently as they did, to answer all their objections, to advise the Methodists not to hear them, to pray constantly and earnestly that God would stop the plague.'[42]

It is not difficult to isolate the main points of agreement and disagreement. These remained remarkably constant from the 1740's to the 1770's, and we may justifiably treat the whole period as doctrinally all of a piece. The Calvinists and Evangelical Arminians were united in ascribing salvation to the free grace of God. Certainly none could legitimately (though some did actually!) mistake Wesley for a Pelagian. This, at any rate, is so as far as his intentions were concerned, though, no doubt, his language was sometimes ambiguous. Dorner was quite right to remark that 'Methodism was on the whole far more removed, as far as saving doctrines were concerned, from Arminianism, than from the old Reformed System'.[43] Again, the strict Calvinist Hodge justly appraised the situation thus:

'Wesleyanism (1) admits entire moral depravity; (2) denies
that men in this state have any power to co-operate with
God; (3) asserts that the guilt of all through Adam was
removed by the justification of all through Christ; (4)
ability to co-operate is of the Holy Spirit, through the
universal influence of the redemption of Christ. The order
of the decrees is (1) to permit the fall of man; (2) to send
the Son to be a full satisfaction for the sins of the whole
world; (3) on that ground to remit all original sin, and to
give such grace as would enable all to attain eternal life;
(4) those who improve that grace and persevere to the end
are ordained to be saved.'[44]

In Hodge's last sentence we see a profound modification of
Arminius by his disciple Wesley, whose set purpose was to
revert to the religious insights of the Dutchman whilst
shunning his rationalistic disciples. With his emphasis that all
is of grace, Wesley represents the high peak of Evangelical
Arminianism. So it was, for example, that in the 1771—4
edition of his *Works* he emphasised the following passage of
his sermon on 'The Means of Grace' by using an asterisk:

' "By grace ye are saved". Ye are saved from your sins,
from the guilt and power thereof, ye are restored to the
favour and image of God, not for any works, *merits* or
deservings of yours, but by the free *grace,* the mere mercy
of God, through the *merits* of his well-beloved Son.'[45]

At first glance there is nothing here with which a Calvinist
would disagree. Indeed, in a letter written to John Newton on
14th May 1765 he said, 'I think on justification just as I have
done at any time these seven-and-twenty years and just as Mr.
Calvin does. In *this* respect, I do not differ from him an hair's
breadth.'[46] But when we probe further into the context of
Wesley's utterances we find that if the issue was not 'grace
versus works' (and that it was not clears Wesley of the charge
of Pelagianism), the question of the nature of grace *as free*
was at the heart of the dispute. Whereas to Wesley 'free
grace' meant grace freely available to all, to Whitefield and
the Calvinists free grace is *given or withheld freely by God.*
Clearly, behind the terminological argument there lies Wesley's
horror of the Calvinistic doctrine of reprobation, and

Whitefield's fear that the logic of Wesley's universalism would lead to a situation in which God's sovereignty would be threatened by man's ability to hold him to ransom and so to frustrate his purposes. Thus, whereas both men upheld the doctrine of total depravity, Wesley maintained man's capacity to respond to God's grace, and this led to Whitefield's protest: 'You plainly make salvation depend not on God's *free-grace,* but on man's *free-will;* and if thus, it is more than probable, Jesus Christ would not have had the satisfaction of seeing the fruit of his death in the eternal salvation of one soul. Our preaching would then be in vain, and all invitations for people to believe in him, would also be in vain.'[47] As Cunningham later put it:

'One great objection to the Arminian doctrine, — that men, even when a divine power amply *sufficient* to produce in them faith and regeneration, has been put forth, may still overcome and frustrate the exercise of this power, and continue unconverted, — is just this, that this doctrine, with whatever general professions about man's depravity and moral impotency by nature, and about the necessity of the gracious operation of the Spirit in producing conversion, it may be accompanied, practically assigns to men themselves, and not to God, the regulating or determining power in the matter, — the power by which, in each case, it *is settled* that repentance and conversion shall take place, — that is that a man shall be put in actual possession of all spiritual blessings, and finally of the kingdom of heaven.'[48]

Again, when Wesley entertained the idea that whilst God did not foreordain, but simply foreknew (yet another idea which his mother so patiently taught him),[49] Whitefield expressed surprise that he could *deny* the doctrine of election by reference to *Romans* 8, wherein it is positively asserted;[50] and in another connection Toplady repeated the standard Calvinistic defence:

'To say, that "events may be foreknown, without falling under any effective or permissive decree"; would be saying either nothing to the purpose, or worse than nothing. For, if God can, with certainty, foreknow any event whatever, which he did not previously determine to accomplish or permit; and that event, barely foreknown but entirely undecreed, be so certainly future, as to furnish positive ground for unerring prophecy; it would follow, (1) That God is dependent, for his knowledge, on the things unknown; instead of all things being dependent on him: and, (2) That there is some extraneous concatenation of causes, prior to the will and knowledge of God, by which his will is regulated, and on which his knowledge is founded. Thus Arminianism, in flying from the decree, jumps over head and ears into the most dangerous and exceptional part of that very stoicism which she pretends to execrate and avoid.'[51]

Needless to say, Wesley remained unconvinced. Indeed, it is not too much to say that Calvinism stuck in his gullet. In his sermon on *Free Grace* (which was omitted by him from his standard *Sermons* on account of its manner) he wrote,

'Sing, O hell, and rejoice ye that are under the earth. For God, even the mighty God, hath spoken and doomed to death thousands of souls, from the rising of the sun to the going down thereof. Here, O death, is thy sting. They shall not, cannot escape. For the mouth of the Lord hath spoken. Here, O grave, is thy victory. Nations yet unborn, or ever they have done good or evil, are doomed never to see the light of life, but thou shalt gnaw upon them for ever and ever. Let all those morning stars sing together who fell with Lucifer, son of the morning. Let all the sons of hell shout for joy. For the degree is past and who shall disannul it?'[52]

Charles Wesley was no less vitriolic in some of his verses. The supreme example, in which he scores a point by misconstruing Calvin's 'horribile' (strictly, 'awe inspiring') is this:

'God, ever merciful and just,
With new-born babes did Tophet fill;
Down into endless torments thrust;
    Merely to show His sovereign will.
This is that *Horrible Decree!*
    This is that wisdom from beneath!
God (O detest the blasphemy!)
    Hath pleasure in the sinner's death.'[53]

John Wesley kept up the fight to the end. In his pamphlet against Toplady's *Life of Zanchy,* he wrote, 'Call it therefore by whatever name you please, Election, Preterition, Predestination or Reprobation, it comes in the end to the same thing. The sense of all is plainly this: By virtue of an eternal, unchangeable, irresistible decree of God, one part of mankind are infallibly saved and the rest infallibly damned; it being impossible that any of the former should be damned, or that any of the latter should be saved. But if this be so, then is all preaching vain'.[54] In a word, he regarded Calvinism as the 'direct antidote to Methodism' for it 'strikes at the root of salvation from sin'. For his part, Whitefield testified, 'I embrace the Calvinistic scheme, not because Calvin, but because Jesus Christ has taught it to me':[55]

'I bless God His Spirit has convinced me of our eternal election by the Father through the Son, of our free justification through faith in His blood, of our sanctification as the consequence of that, and of our final perseverance and glorification as the result of all. These I am persuaded God has joined together; these, neither men nor devils shall ever be able to put asunder.'[56]

It was in the light of such views that Whitefield replied to Wesley's sermon of Free Grace. He argued that far from preaching's being superfluous if Calvinism be true, 'since we know not who are elect, and who reprobate, we are to preach promiscuously to all. For the word may be useful, even to the non-elect in restraining them from much wickedness and sin'.[57] Further, far from militating against holy living, Calvinism makes holiness a 'mark of our election'.[58] Nor does the doctrine of predestination destroy our happiness; on the contrary, as the XVIIth Anglican Article states, that doctrine 'is full of sweet, pleasant, unspeakable comforts to godly persons'[59] — a position this which Wesley could never comprehend. As to the number of the damned, no Calvinist has ever held what Wesley alleges, namely, that 'thousands and millions of men, without any preceding offence or fault of theirs, were unchangeably doomed to everlasting burnings'. We must not overlook man's nature as *fallen,* nor forget that 'God might justly have passed them *all* by, without sending his own Son to be a saviour for any one'.[60] It is just untrue that God's absolute purpose to save the elect overthrows the Christian religion:

> 'No, dear Sir, you mistake. Infidels of all kinds are on your side of the question. Deists, Arians, Socinians, arraign God's sovereignty, and stand up for universal redemption. I pray God, that dear Mr. Wesley's sermon, as it has grieved the hearts of many of God's children, may not also strengthen the hands of many of his most avowed enemies!'[61]

To reiterate Whitefield's most serious charge: 'You plainly make salvation depend not on God's *free grace,* but on man's *free-will . . .* '[62]

However unlike Pelagius he was in other ways, Wesley concurred with him in the view that Christians ought to live holy lives, and this conviction was a powerful stimulant to his attacks on doctrinal and practical antinomianism. But on this point he and the leading Calvinists were, as we have seen, at one.[63] None of them denied the necessity of good works, though the Calvinists were ever suspicious of any kind of Arminianism which might represent works as being the means to salvation. It was when Wesley went further and propounded his doctrine of perfection — or perfect love, as he preferred to call it — that he and the Calvinists parted company. The latter constantly misunderstood him — and, it must be admitted, the fault was not entirely theirs. Professor Outler has put the happiest construction upon Wesley's intentions in this connection:

> ' "Perfect love", as Wesley understood it, is the conscious certainty, *in the present moment,* of the fulness of one's love for God and neighbor, as this love has been initiated and fulfilled by God's gifts of faith, hope and love. This is not a state but a dynamic process: saving faith is its beginning; sanctification is its proper climax.'[64]

The related notion that man could finally fall away from grace was rightly regarded by Calvinists as an attack upon the doctrine of the final perseverance of the saints, and therefore upon God's competence to bring his saving purposes to pass.

As he completed his review of the Calvinist-Arminian

controversy, the Methodist historian Abel Stevens consoled himself with these words: 'We may retire then from this stormy battle-field, grateful that, amid its din and smoke, we have been able to catch some memorable glimpses of the clear and serene heaven above it.'[65] Bogue and Bennett did not share his confidence:

> 'On looking back to the heat of the controversy, it is painful to reflect that scarcely ever was so important a subject discussed with so bad success . . . With whomsoever the victory might be supposed to rest, acquired by such weapons, it could confer no glory . . . It is as painful as it is remarkable, that the true point on which the whole controversy turns was never brought into view. This could not be expected from the arminians, whose cause it would have injured. But the calvinists, by this neglect, betrayed a want of insight into their own system. The contest, concerning what God designed from eternity, must at last be decided by what he effects in time; for his actions are the ennunciation of his decrees. As Mr. Wesley professed to admit that God was the author of conversion, that he gave the will its right direction, and sustained the religion which he first produced; when this admission is pursued to all its consequences, it proves all that calvinism requires. Instead, however, of discussing this interesting question which lay within their reach . . . the combatants pushed each other back into the ages of eternity, to speculate upon the order of the thoughts which passed in the infinite mind.'[66]

The burden of this judgment — and it is one for which there is much to be said — is that Arminianism of the heart did not so much present a genuine alternative to Calvinism, as an inconsistent deviation from it. Ascribing everything to God's grace as he did, it ought to have been more difficult than it apparently was for Wesley also to hold so strongly to man's ability to spurn, and finally to fall from, that grace; and he ought to have seen more clearly than he did, the emptiness of the view which ascribes foreknowledge to *God,* but denies him foreordaining powers. Further, the idea that Christ actually died for all men does, when pressed as the Arminians pressed it, issue in *reconcilability* for all, but the actual and

certain reconciliation of none. Not surprisingly the Calvinist
Cunningham concluded that 'Pelagian Arminianism is more
consistent with itself than Arminianism in its more evangelical
forms; and there is a strong tendency in systems of doctrine
to develop their true nature and bearings fully and consistently.
Socinianism, indeed, is more consistent than either of them'.[67]
For all that, it must be confessed that the Wesleyan protest
against a God of capricious partiality was and remains a
standing challenge to Calvinists to present their case with due
care and humility, and, in the interests of morality, to see that
the Cross is never far from their thoughts on the matter.

We are left, then, with two parties to a dispute, both of
whom wished to extol saving grace; and on either side of the
divide there were those who feared that their opponents were
in danger of distorting the gospel.[68] If the Calvinists jealously
guarded God's sovereignty and justice the Arminians accused
them of threatening his love. If the Arminians emphasised
man's ethical responsibilities *some* Calvinists accused them of
(at best) Semi-Pelagianism. The universalism of the Arminians
made the Cross as superfluous to the Calvinists as *their*
election, whose seat was in the inscrutable will of God, made
it to the Arminians. The entire episode manifests the disrup-
tions which can be caused by those whose minds, fanned by
religious zeal, and partially, no doubt, clouded by 'non-
theological' factors, operate by way of strong disjunctions
and are, to that extent, blinkered.

We have yet to mention John Wesley's greatest anti-
Calvinistic work, *Predestination Calmly Considered* (1752).[69]
In it he laid down the main lines of his position as we have
already described it. Our reason for withholding mention of
the book until now is that we are thus able to point out that
the work connects Wesley with that other stream of Calvinist
witness — that of the Particular Baptists. For a considerable
part of Wesley's statement here is in direct reply to Dr. John
Gill (1697–1771).[70] The redoubtable Gill engaged in numerous
controversies during the course of his London ministry, which
lasted from 1719–71. He defended the doctrine of the
Trinity against Arianism; he belaboured the paedo-baptists
with arguments against their position and in favour of his
own; but the disputes which chiefly concern us are those

in which he battled against antinomianism and Arminianism. It is a tribute to the forcefulness of Gill's writing, and an indication of the theological stances of his commentators, that bold and contradictory judgments have been passed upon him. Leaving on one side Benjamin Francis's 'An Elegy on the Death of Dr. John Gill',[71] in which we are informed that the 'transparent breast' of 'heav'n-taught Gill' shone

'With light divine, imbib'd from the sole fount
Of evangelic and celestial truth . . .'

we may note the opinion of Gill's friend Toplady to the effect that 'While true Religion, and sound Learning, have a single friend remaining in the British Empire, the *Works* and Name of Gill will be *precious* and revered'.[72] Likewise, Walter Wilson did not doubt that Gill, 'for the value and extent of his writings will be considered by future generations as one of the Fathers of the Church'[73] — a prophecy which it cannot be said has widely been fulfilled. On the other hand, John Fawcett (1740–1817), a Particular Baptist who tended to avoid rather than to delight in doctrinal disputation, replied in verse when reprimanded for being insufficiently Gill-like in his preaching:

'To be brief, my dear friends, you may say what you will,
I'll ne'er be confined to read nothing but Gill.'[74]

This from the man who, having supplied the aged and infirm Gill's pulpit, declined the invitation to succeed him in response, so it is said, to the importunate appeals of his lowly flock at Wainsgate. Certainly they did so plead; but there may well have been theological overtones to Fawcett's refusal of the pastorate — thereby making way for Gill's biographer, John Rippon. Undoubtedly Fawcett lamented the taste for polemic divinity which had been nourished by Gill and his supporters.[75] Robert Hall (1764–1831) expressed his opinion in even more pungent terms when the Welsh Calvinist Christmas Evans lamented the fact that Gill's works had not been written in Welsh. Hall expostulated, 'I wish they had, sir; I wish they had, with all my heart, sir, for then I should never have read them! They are a continent of mud, sir!'[76] In our own century Dr. Whitley spoke with slightly mocking humour of Gill and his colleague John Brine (1703–65),

saying that 'Gill was drowned in Hebrew except when he woke
to fulminate at Wesley . . . Brine was at Carriers' Hall exag-
gerating hyper-Calvinism till he had only thirty of the elect
left'.[77] However, as Dr. Horton Davies has more recently
reminded us, Gill's people loved him, and 'the church was
prepared to raise a mortgage and go into debt in order to have
a portrait made of Dr. Gill, from which mezzo-tints might be
provided for every member of the congregation'.[78] Among
those who to this day have a high regard for John Gill is the
American philosopher Dr. Gordon H. Clark.[79]

It is not difficult to trace the theological pedigree of Gill
and Brine. They were both indebted to the ministry of John
Skepp. He had taken part in Gill's ordination in 1720; he
had been Brine's predecessor at Currier's Hall; it was by
Skepp that Gill was encouraged in his Hebrew studies, and
after Skepp's death Gill purchased many of his books. Above
all, Skepp had been a member of Hussey's church at Cambridge
and his own theological stance is adequately described by the
title of his book published in 1722, and republished by Gill
in 1751; *The divine energy: or the efficacious operations of
the Spirit of God in the soul of man, in his effectual calling
and conversion: stated, proved, and vindicated. Wherein the
real weakness and insufficiency of moral persuasion, without
the super-addition of the exceeding greatness of God's power
for faith and conversion to God, are fully evinced. Being an
antidote against the Pelagian plague.* So persuaded was Skepp
that God must have all the glory, and that man could do
nothing, that he, like Hussey before him, refused to *offer* the
gospel lest it be thought that any but God's Holy Spirit could
apply it to the heart, or that sinful man had the moral ability
to respond. This was the position which Gill and Brine
strenuously defended against the supporters of Mathias
Maurice of Rothwell.

Fourteen years after his arrival in England from Wales
Maurice wrote a defence of the pro-High Calvinist Henllan
secession, but in 1737, after a complete theological *volte face,*
he published *The Modern Question.* He here forsook High
Calvinism, and proclaimed the duty of hearers of the Word to
believe in Christ. Lewis Wayman of Kimbolton countered with
A further enquiry after truth (1738), and in the same year

Maurice died. His posthumously published *The modern question affirm'd and proved* (1739) carried a preface written by the London minister, Thomas Bradbury, and Dr. Nuttall points out that the significance of this is that the controversy now reached the metropolis.[80] There the arch opponents of Maurice were Gill and Brine; perhaps his most illustrious supporter was Philip Doddridge who, by 1747, was raising the question of world mission.[81] Wilson stated the crucial issue baldly: 'In one point [Gill] differed from most of his brethren. It was not his practice to address unconverted sinners, nor to enforce the invitations of the gospel.'[82] Gill's fear, of course, was of a widespread lapse into Arminian universalism. Indeed, even before the modern question was opened he had, in 1732, an exchange with Abraham Taylor over the Calvinist-Arminian issue;[83] and when, in 1735, Taylor published *The Modern Question Concerning Repentance and Faith Examined* — a book which was later to make such a favourable impression on Andrew Fuller — Brine replied, though not until 1743, in his *A refutation of Arminian principles, etc.* Gill had meanwhile been answering the Arminianism of Dr. Whitby (1638–1726)[84] in his *The Cause of God and Truth* (1735–8).

Like many High Calvinists before them Gill and Brine were accused of antinomianism; and like most High Calvinists they were blameless as far as practical antinomianism was concerned.[85] Gill would have none of it: 'For my part I have been traduced as an Antinomian, for innocently asserting that the essence of justification . . . lies in the will of God — I *abhor* the thoughts of setting the law of God aside as the rule of walk and conversation; and constantly affirm . . . that all who believe in Christ for righteousness should be careful to maintain good works, for necessary uses.'[86] Although Gill might be thought to have added fuel to the fire by republishing Crisp's *Works* in 1755, thereby giving a further lease of life to what John Fletcher was to call 'Crispianity', his avowed intention was to *clear* Crisp of the charge of antinomianism by annotating the works. He had to admit, however, that Crisp had been ill advised to speak of believers as being immune from sin, and whilst taking him to mean that believers have already been freed by Christ as far as their

eternal estate is concerned, he advocated the avoidance of such
ambiguous language.[87] Brine's part in the anti-antinomian conflict is illustrated by the posthumous *The Moral Law the Rule
of Moral Conduct to Believers, considered and enforced by
arguments extracted from the judicious Mr. Brine's 'Certain
Efficacy of the Death of Christ'* (1792). Others conducted
their case in more poetic vein, and since so much doctrine
has been promulgated amongst nonconformists *via* the hymnal,
it may not be inappropriate to quote a verse by the Calvinist
Joseph Hart (1712—68)[88] who, in one verse (not, admittedly,
his greatest) opposes doctrinal aridity and advocates a warm
experimental faith; opposes antinomianism and the disputa-
tious spirit; and testifies to the necessity of regeneration by
the Holy Spirit:

'No big words of ready talkers,
    No dry doctrine will suffice;
Broken hearts, and humble walkers,
    These are dear in Jesus' eyes.
Tinkling sounds of disputation,
    Naked knowledge, all are vain;
Every soul that gains salvation
    Must and shall be born again.'

So much for the battles of Gill and his colleagues. Now to
come to his more positive points. Gill was an unyielding
covenant theologian in the line of Witsius, for whom he had
great respect. This is evidenced by his *magnum opus A Body
of Doctrinal* [1767] and [N.B.] *Practical Divinity* (1770), on
which work he did not embark until he had completed his
twelve-volume commentary on the Bible. But much earlier in
his ministry he had expressed the kernel of his system in his
Declaration of Faith and [N.B.] *Practice*[89] from which we
take the following extracts:

'We believe, that before the world began, God did elect a
certain number of men unto everlasting Salvation whom he
did predestinate to the adoption of children by Jesus of
his own free grace & according to the good pleasure of his
will, & that in pursuance of this gratious design, he did
contrive & make a covenant of grace and peace with his Son
Jesus Christ, on ye behalf of those persons, wherein a

Saviour was appointed, & all spiritual blessings provided for them; as also that their persons with all their grace & glory, were put into ye hands of Christ, & made his care & charge . . . We believe, yt that Eternal Redemption which Christ has obtained by the shedding of his blood, is special & particular . . . that the Justification of God's Elect, is onely by the righteousness of Christ imputed to them, without ye consideration of any works of righteousness done by them . . . yt the work of regeneration, conversion, sanctification, & faith is not an act of man's free will & power, but of the mighty, efficacious & irresistible grace of God . . . that all those who are chosen by the father, redeemed by the son & sanctified by the spirit shall certainly & finally persevere, so yt none of 'em shall ever perish, but shall have everlasting life.'

A number of emphases here placed Gill over against Wesley, and we shall comment upon two of them. In 1752 Gill published *The Doctrine of the Saint's Final Perseverance* in reply to Wesley's *Serious Thoughts on the Perseverance of the Saints.* Unlike Arminius himself, Wesley was in no doubt that the Calvinist doctrine of perseverance was untenable, and that it conduced to antinomianism. Gill replied, as any Calvinist would, that it is inconceivable that any of the elect shall finally be lost. Then Wesley brought out his *Predestination Calmly Considered,* and here shifted the discussion to that feature of Calvinism which most appalled him, reprobation: 'Find out any election which does not imply reprobation and I will gladly agree to it. But reprobation I can never agree to while I believe the Scripture to be of God; as being utterly irreconcilable to the whole scope and tenor both of the Old and New Testament.'[90] Dr. Outler remarks, 'This is the nub of Wesley's protest. He belabours the point, for he regarded the arbitrary damnation of any man with such horror that he ignores all else in the opposing argument.'[91] Wesley's omissions did not go unnoticed by Gill, who made a prompt reply, nor by later Calvinists such as Cunningham, who complained that both Wesley, and Whitby in his *Five Points,* had unduly emphasised reprobation, and had failed entirely to take the force of the Calvinist insistence on stating election positively (since there is more scriptural evidence for it), and on regarding reprobation as a legitimate, less fully scripturally authenticated, deduction from it.[92] With the Westminster Confession Gill attributes both election and reprobation to God's secret will, whereas the tendency in Calvin was to relate election to God's secret will, and reprobation to his manifest will displayed on account of man's sin. Wesley returned to the fray with a poem of thirty-seven stanzas entitled *An Answer to all which the Rev. Dr. Gill has printed on the Final perseverance of the Saints* (1754).[93] None was more delighted by Gill's performance in the contest than Toplady, whose recollection of the episode is illuminating:

> 'Between morning and afternoon service, read through Dr. Gill's excellent and nervous tract on Predestination, against Wesley. How sweet is that blessed and glorious doctrine to the soul, when it is received through the channel of inward experience! I remember, a few years ago, Mr. Wesley said to me, concerning Dr. Gill, "he is a positive man, and fights for his own opinions through thick and thin". Let the Doctor fight as he will, I'm sure he fights to good purpose: and, I believe it may be said of my learned friend, as it was of the Duke of Marlborough, that he never fought a battle which did not win'[94]

No matter how much we may respect Gill for his prodigious labours (and, incidentally, agree with Bogue and Bennett that 'he seems to inquire how much, rather than how well he could write on every subject')[95] the fact remains that for all his assertion of the need to *declare* the gospel,[96] he does seem to have underemphasised the gospel *call*. As E. F. Clipsham properly notes, 'Gill . . . went to great lengths to explain away the meaning of "all" wherever it occurs in connection with the universal proclamation of the gospel, and studiously avoided the direct commands and exhortations in the Bible, to repent and believe on Christ and be saved.'[97] This inhibiting factor led, and was later to lead, to undue introspection at the expense of Christ-centredness — for if the gospel is for 'sensible sinners' only, I must continually ascertain whether or not I fall into that class with a view to making sure that I have a *warrant* to believe the gospel. Wayman of Kimbolton took this view, as did William Gadsby (1773–1844),[98] who carried this significant modification of Gill's approach to faith into the nineteenth century, and whose followers today are chiefly to be found among the Gospel Standard Baptists.[99] Though loved by his flock Gill was, as J. C. Ryland discovered in 1753, ministering to 153 hearers in a meeting house whose seating capacity was 2,000.[100] Concurrently, the *Calvinist* Whitefield was preaching to thousands. It is not that numbers are everything, but it does seem that the latter was casting his net wider than the former, and that this indicates a markedly different understanding of Christian mission. J. M. Cramp aptly summarised the approach of Gill and Brine as follows:

> 'They were supra-lapsarians, holding that God's election was irrespective of the fall of man. They taught eternal justifica-tion. Undue prominence was given in their discourses to the teachings of scripture teaching the divine purposes . . . They were satisfied with stating men's danger, and assuring them that they were on the high road to perdition. But they did not call upon them to repent and believe the gospel. They did not entreat them to be reconciled unto God . . . And the churches did not, could not, under their instruc-tion, engage in efforts for the conversion of souls. They were so afraid of intruding on God's work that they neglected to do what he had commanded them.'[101]

It would be wrong to conclude that 'Gillism' (as it came to be known in contradistinction to 'Fullerism') was the sole cause for what is variously termed the 'blight' or the 'chill' which was to come upon the Particular Baptists. Many of them were more than a little suspicious of methodism of all kinds (as Watts had been); and even Andrew Fuller (1754–1815),[102] in a letter to William Ward dated 21st September 1800, could exhort him to 'Shun all asperity, and low wit such as our Methodists effect'.[103] However, *some* Particular Baptists had never ceased to proclaim Christ freely, and it would be as unjust to them to suggest that Fuller unaided lit the torch of mission, as it would be to Gill to accuse him of being solely responsible for the evangelistic lethargy of his times.

Among those Baptists who partook of the evangelistic spirit[104] we may mention, in order of seniority, Alvery Jackson, pastor at Barnoldswick from 1718–63.[105] That he

held faith and works in balance is clearly seen in one of his
hymns:

> 'Sinners are saved by Grace
>   And works excluded are;
> But where true saving grace doth work,
>   Good works the product are.'

Even more important was his publication, in 1752, of *The
Question Answered, Whether saving Faith in Christ is a Duty
required by the moral law of all those who live under the
Gospel Revelation.* He here declared that preachers are obliged
to offer Christ promiscuously, and that hearers are obliged to
receive him. In London, Andrew Gifford (1700–84)[106] aroused
the ire of some of his fellow Baptists by befriending Whitefield.
He was present at the stone-laying ceremony of Whitefield's
Tabernacle in 1756; he subsequently preached there, and
later still he edited Whitefield's sermons. His tract *The Living
Water* (1746) was an earnest appeal to sinners to seek the
Lord. Worthy of note also is Benjamin Beddome (1717–95),
pastor for over half a century at Bourton-on-the-Water —
despite earnest entreaties that he should accept calls elsewhere.[107] Among over forty converts added to the Bourton
membership roll in 1741 was John Collett Ryland (1723–92),
notorious for his reply to William Carey's request to discuss
the question of the missionary obligation: 'Young man, sit
down. You're an enthusiast'.[108] Beddome speaks for Jackson,
Gifford and himself when, in his sermon of 'The Heavenly
Calling' he writes, 'The general call is to all that come under
the sound of the gospel . . . Ministers stand at the door and
knock; the Spirit comes with his key and opens the door'.[109]
It will not escape notice that Beddome, the youngest of our
examples, was born thirty-seven years before Fuller. Such
men were, however, in the minority.

With the appearance in 1770 of a Circular Letter issued by
the Northamptonshire Association we detect a distinct change
of key: 'Every soul that comes to Christ to be saved from
hell and sin by him, is to be encouraged . . .'[110] It is not
surprising that such a statement should have come from
Northamptonshire, for, as Dr. Whitley relates, a number of
evangelical Calvinists had made the East Midlands the scene of
their labours:

'Joshua Burton had brought to Foxton something learned from Abraham Booth at Sutton-in-Ashfield. From the delightful village of Bourton-on-the-water . . . had come first the Rylands . . . and more lately Alexander Payne . . . The coming of John Goodrich from Preston shows that Stony Stratford had before 1790 passed over to the Particulars. And Lancashire had sent also John Law, from Rossendale . . . Barnoldswick, in Yorkshire, had contributed Abraham Greenwood [who had been converted under Alvery Jackson] . . . His fellow-student, John Sutcliff . . . was settled for his life work at Olney. And at Nottingham, again of General Baptist origin, was to be found Richard Hopper . . .'[111]

Pre-eminent, however, was Robert Hall (1728–91),[112] who came to Arnesby in 1753, and who delivered a sermon before the Northamptonshire Association in 1779 which was afterwards expanded to become *Help to Zion's Travellers* (1781). Herein he declared that 'The way to Jesus is graciously laid open for every one who chooses to come to him'.

Meanwhile, Fuller, brought up under Gillism, had been agonising over theological matters, and in particular, that of eternal justification. Gill and Brine had inherited this view from Crisp, and Brine had defended it in his *Motives to Love and Unity* and *A Defence of the Doctrine of Eternal Justification.* Again, his reading of Bunyan and Erskine perplexed him in view of their clear and indiscriminate offer of the gospel to sinners. At first he sided with Gill and Brine, but shortly after his ordination at Kettering in October 1783, Abraham Taylor's *The Modern Question* and John Martin's *The Rock of Offence* came his way, and he was persuaded by the former in favour of the free offer, and by the latter, that it was the duty of hearers of the gospel to close with Christ. His evangelical thoughts were further nourished by his contacts with John Sutcliff, John Ryland and Robert Hall, all of whom had been influenced by Jonathan Edwards. Hall introduced Fuller to Edwards's *Inquiry into the Freedom of the Will,* which work he read in 1777 (having first mistaken Hall's advice and read *Veritas Redux* by John Edwards of Cambridge). Fuller gradually came to appreciate the force of the distinction between sinful man's actual responsibility, and yet his moral inability, to heed God's call. Hall's own *Help to Zion's Travellers* was a further stimulus to Fuller's evangelicalism. Further works of Jonathan Edwards persuaded him that faith is cleaving to Christ; that internal warrants to believe are beside the point; and that (*pace* Gill) Christ's righteousness is figuratively and not actually imputed to the believer. Fuller set out his position in 1781 in *The Gospel Worthy of All Acceptation, Or the Obligations of Men fully to credit and cordially to approve whatever God makes known.*[113] First written by way of personal stock-taking, the work was not published until 1785. The stir which it caused, and the influence which it had upon Carey, are legendary. As early as 30th August 1780 Fuller had written,

> 'We shackle ourselves too much in our addresses to sinners; that we have bewildered and lost ourselves by taking the decrees of God as rules of action. Surely Peter and Paul never felt such scruples in their addresses as we do.'[114]

And in the Confession of Faith which he devised at the time of his ordination at Kettering, Fuller set his face against both Socinianism and Arminianism; upheld the doctrine of election, and conceived of reprobation as God's 'determination to punish sin in certain cases in the person of the sinner'; asserted regeneration by the Holy Spirit as the *sine qua non* of conversion, and maintained the doctrine of the perseverance of the saints. He continued,

> 'I believe it is the duty of every minister of Christ plainly and faithfully to preach the Gospel to all who will hear it; and as I believe the inability of men to spiritual things to be wholly of the *moral,* and therefore of the criminal kind, and that it is their duty to love the Lord Jesus Christ and trust in him for salvation though they do not; I therefore believe free and solemn addresses, invitations, calls, and warnings to them to be not only *consistent,* but directly *adapted,* as means, in the hand of the Spirit of God, to bring them to Christ. I consider it as a part of my duty which I could not omit without being guilty of the blood of souls'.[115]

Like Whitefield before them Fuller and his colleagues were accused of Arminianism — both by Arminians such as Dan

Taylor, who thought that the logical consequence of Fullerism was an accession of strength to his own New Connexion of General Baptists; and by Calvinists in the line of Hussey and Gill who saw, in the gospel offer, an Arminianising tendency which could only detract from God's sovereignty in salvation, and foster unworthy synergistic notions. Thus, Dan Taylor published *Observations on the Gospel Worthy of all Acceptation* (1786) under the pseudonym 'Philanthropos'; William Button attacked from the High Calvinist side and so, even more significantly, did the very John Martin (1741—1820), who had penned the Northamptonshire Circular Letter of 1770, whose *Rock of Offence* had so appealed to Fuller in 1775, but who had now undergone a change of heart in the opposite direction to that of Maurice some years before. Even Abraham Booth, in general Fuller's supporter, accused him in 1802 of holding inadequate views on inspiration, substitution and general redemption.[116] This last point was particularly important in view of the charge of Arminianism which was laid against Fuller. We must ever remember that he opposed universalism (his opposition to William Vidler, the erstwhile Particular Baptist who succeeded Elhanan Winchester as leader of Britain's universalists was strenuous); and that when he emphasised the sufficiency of Christ's death and God's ability to save all the world if he had so desired, he was combating a quasi-quantitative view of Christ's atoning work according to which Christ had suffered for exactly the number of sins committed by those who were to be saved. On the more general point he wrote to Ryland: 'Mr. [Richard] Baxter considers Calvinists and Arminians as reconcilable . . . I have no such idea; and if . . . I were disowned by my present connexions, I should choose to go through the world alone than be connected with them.' By his own estimation Fuller was a strict Calvinist. As he said, 'I do not believe every thing that Calvin taught, nor any thing because he taught it; but I reckon strict Calvinism to be my own system'.[117] Certainly Calvin was not averse to offering the gospel freely.[118]

CHAPTER FOUR

Running into the Sand

The debate rumbled on into the nineteenth century, attracting a decreasing number of participants, and a decreasing amount of attention. No doubt Wesley was somewhat premature when, in the first issue of the *Arminian Magazine* (1778) he wrote, 'Whatsoever was the case in times past, very few now receive [the Decrees] even in Holland. And in Geneva they are universally rejected with the utmost horror. The case is nearly the same in England'.[1] However, it is interesting to observe that in 1798 the name of the magazine was changed to the less provocative *Methodist Magazine,* and in the same year John Eyre wrote that 'Calvinists and Wesleyans have ceased to irritate each other'.[2] The credit for the change of mood goes in part to such men as Edward Williams (1750–1813), whose writings smoothed the corners of extremer Calvinism, and whose influence as Principal of Rotherham Academy from 1795 to his death was considerable.[3] He defined Modern Calvinism as 'That system of religion which represents the sovereignty of Divine grace, without encroaching on the equity of Divine government'; and Modern Arminianism as 'That system of religion which represents the equity of Divine Government in such a manner as to encroach on the sovereignty of Divine Grace'.[4] That Calvinists did not always have an easy ride when they sought to modify the Calvinism of their fathers is illustrated by the experience of William Roby (1766–1830), who wrote of his Reading days:

'I had been accustomed to deny that the law was the believer's rule of life, that he had anything to do with the law, etc. By the law I understood merely the covenant of works. At Reading I began to discover the practical effects of this unguarded mode of expression. This led me to examine it more particularly. Fisher's *Marrow of Modern Divinity*, with Boston's notes, were very useful at this time. I began to point out the erroneous and dangerous mode of expression. This produced a ferment in the congregation who petitioned for my removal.'[5]

Later, at Wigan, when his brother-in-law Mr. Gilbert began exalting grace after the manner of William Huntington, by whom he had been influenced, Roby found that two opposing parties grew up within the church: 'For upwards of two years, I scarcely ever preached a sermon which was not reproached by one party as Arminian, and by the other as Antinomian'.[6] Such difficulties notwithstanding, the future was with Roby, and the Congregational Union's Declaration of 1833 significantly modified the doctrinal position of the denomination as stated in the Savoy Declaration of 1658. So much so that Richard Winter Hamilton of Leeds declared, 'I do fear that there is creeping among us a refining method as to the great propoundings of the gospel. The full-blooded dogma of the old school must be revived . . . Our Congregational Union symbol of faith is to me unsatisfactory and lamentable'.[7] But Hamilton was swimming against the tide.

A similar relaxation of the hold on things Calvinistic was taking place in Wales and Scotland. True, in 1800 there was a market for Timothy Jones's reissued *Y Wisg Wen Ddysglaer* (1759), in which views akin to those of Gill were propounded; and John Elias (1774–1841) could still maintain the evangelical version of High Calvinism:

'I think that the sound doctrine that is generally called Calvinism is much misrepresented: the Hyper-Calvinists give occasion to the doctrine called *Antinomianism*.

I do not know how those that deny the *total* corruption of the human nature, and that salvation as to its plan, its performance, its application, is of grace only, can be considered as faithful ministers. On the other hand, I cannot understand how those that are against calling, inviting, persuading, and compelling sinners to come to Christ, can be said to preach the Gospel. I believe that declining to preach the Gospel to every creature is contrary to the Word of God, and inconsistent with sound doctrine.'[8]

Fullerism and other varieties of moderate Calvinism were meanwhile making themselves felt in Wales, and among those influenced by them was John Roberts of Llanbrynmair (1767–1834), a student of the works of Jonathan Edwards, Edward Williams (who had conducted an academy at Oswestry), and Fuller himself. For a time the celebrated Calvinistic Baptist preacher Christmas Evans (1766–1838) embraced Fullerism, but he subsequently reverted to the Gillite stance he had adopted in his *Neilltuolrwydd y Prynedigaeth* (1811), a work of similar import to *Y Palas Arian* (1811) by the influential John Jenkins of Hengoed. In 1823 the Welsh Calvinistic Methodists adopted a Confession of Faith based on the Westminster Confession, but eventually, after controversies in the 1820's and 30's moderatism gained the upper hand in the Principality.[9]

The decline of High Calvinism and the emergence of Arminianism in Scotland did not come about painlessly. The Relief Synod (1761) had from the outset denounced antinomianism and expressed sympathy with Whitefield's evangelical Calvinism. Among the Congregationalists Ralph Wardlaw (1779–1853) sponsored Amyraldism and advocated a position similar to that of Edward Williams. For doing the same thing John Brown (Tertius) found himself in controversy with the United Secession Synod (1820), and eventually James Morison (1816–93) was forced to leave that body for the sake of views which came to be incorporated in the doctrinal formulae of the Evangelical Union, which Morison and his supporters founded in 1843. The distinctive tenets of the Evangelical Union are enshrined in its Declaration of 1858, from which we select two sample statements: 'in opposition to the scheme of a necessitated will as held, not by Calvinists only, but (as would appear) by all classes of infidels, the E.U. Conference holds tenaciously to the doctrine of free will as lying at the foundation of all religion, natural and revealed . . . No inconsistency, then, can be greater than that of maintaining that the Son died for all, and that his atonement expressed the Father's love for all, while at the same time, it is contended that the needed influence of the Spirit stops short of all, and embraces those only who are included in the circle of the unconditionally elect.'[10] Kindred views were espoused by the Congregationalist poet George Macdonald (1824–1905), and by his ministerial colleague John Kirk who, in 1842, found himself at the centre of controversy because of his desire to go beyond Wardlaw's Amyraldism in the direction of Arminianism. Cunningham was in no doubt of the identity of the real patron of all such movements:

> 'We have had in our day, and among ourselves, a grossly Pelagian Arminianism, which manifested for a time a considerable measure of active and ardent zeal . . . The atonement, with them, is reduced to being little or nothing else practically . . . than a mere exhibition and proof of God's love to men . . . while the view they give of man's natural power to believe the gospel . . . contradicts the plain doctrine of Scripture concerning the depravity of human nature, and practically supersedes the necessity of the special efficacious agency of the Holy Spirit in the production of faith and conversion.'[11]

Within the Scottish Presbyterian Establishment the lay theologian Thomas Erskine of Linlathen (1788–1870) caused some concern because of his liberal views — especially those indicated by the title of one of his books, *The Unconditional Freeness of the Gospel* (1828); and John McLeod Campbell (1800–72) was excluded from the ministry in 1831 because of views on the universality of the atonement which he subsequently advanced in detail in *The Nature of the Atonement* (1856). The Free Church of Scotland, a separated body since the Disruption of 1843, reaffirmed confessional Calvinism, and stood as a bulwark against what was taken to be an indefensible erosion of doctrine within the Church of Scotland. For those who remained in the latter Church the way was by no means easy. Thus, in the 1850's the distinguished philosopher-theologian John Caird (1820–98), then a pastor, wrote that 'The horrible spirit of Church bigotry and narrow-souled orthodoxy is now so rampant, that any sort of preaching that does not bear the broad stamp of orthodox mintage in tone and language is apt to be looked upon with a very suspicious eye'.[12] As he looked back upon the latter part of the nineteenth century, and such exceptions as John Kennedy of Dingwall (1819—84) apart, Dr. Macleod had to conclude that

> 'It was, however, the day of ebb-tide and the definite out-and-out Calvinism of another day was going out of fashion and yielding place to a presentation of the Gospel which, without being pronouncedly Arminian, avoided the emphasis which the older Evangelicals laid on the New Birth as a Divine intervention. This modified message put its emphasis on the need the sinner has of forgiveness to the eclipse of the equally urgent need that he has of regeneration . . . In this connection the newer Evangelicalism said less of the Spirit and His work and of the provision made in Christ for a walk in newness of life than did the fuller message which brought home as equally urgent the need of having a man's nature renewed with that of having acceptance for his person.'[13]

None were more zealous in pursuing Arminianism and antinomianism *amongst themselves* as the English Calvinistic Baptists. We have already referred to William Gadsby who, though accused by some of doctrinal antinomianism, never ceased to advocate the necessity of good works as a fruit of faith, and was more productive of schemes for Sunday school teaching, social welfare, and the like, than most of his co-religionists — and all this *despite* his refusal to 'offer' the gospel. Indeed, Gadsby considered Fuller to be 'the greatest enemy the church of God ever had, as his sentiments were so much cloaked with the sheep's clothing'.[14] John Warburton (1776—1857), who ministered for over forty years at Trowbridge, and John Kershaw (1792—1870), pastor for over fifty years to Calvinistic Baptists in Rochdale,[15] both of whom had been converted under Gadsby's ministry at Back Lane, Manchester, were among his prominent sympathisers. James Wells (1803—70) of the Surrey Tabernacle was another who largely shared Gadsby's anti-free-offer views.[16] Gadsby found John Stevens's pamphlet against doctrinal antinomianism inadequate, but was, no doubt, more happily impressed by the same writer's *Help for the True Disciples of Immanuel. being an answer to a book . . . entitled The Gospel Worthy of All Acceptation* (1829), in which Fuller's position on the duty faith question was opposed on the ground than faith cannot be an obligation upon unregenerate men. As for Fuller's alleged Arminianism, in 1807 the Suffolk and Norfolk Association of Strict [communion] and Particular Baptists (founded in 1769) protested that Fullerism tended towards universalism; and in 1831 William Rushton of Liverpool, standing in the line of Hussey, published his *A Defence of Particular Redemption*. He here pointed out that Fuller 'neither teaches that Christ died for His elect only, nor does He affirm that He died for the whole race of Adam, but he maintains that Christ made an atonement for sin indefinitely, for sin in general, in such a way as that God might pardon some men if He pleased, or all men if He pleased. Thus Mr. Fuller denies that the death of Christ is vicarious'.[17] Finally, we may note the comment of the Gospel Standard Baptist leader, J. C. Philpot (1802—69), the erstwhile Anglican parson: 'Had I no other preservative, I think my daily and almost hourly sense of my miserable helplessness and thorough impotency to raise up my soul to one act of faith, hope or love would keep me from assenting to Andrew Fuller's lies. Nothing suits my soul but sovereign, omnipotent, and super-abounding grace. I am no common sinner, and must therefore have no common grace'.[18]

Meanwhile, from the other side, but still within the Baptist fold, John Lind had denounced reprobation and contended for the indiscriminate offer of the gospel in his *An Important Question Answered* (1813); and compatible with this stand were the later statements of such men as Moses Fisher of Liverpool. It was but a short step to the universalism of David Griffiths, tutor at Accrington Academy, whose book *The Atonement of Jesus Christ Explained and Defended* (1837) caused consternation in the more conservative quarters. Certainly not all were able to find their way in the manner advocated by John Hooper of Hoxton in 1819: 'We must not merge the doctrinal in the practical preacher; to avoid the gulphs of antinomianism, we must not dash against the rocks of arminianism; the golden mean lies between, and happy is he who is enabled to maintain it.'[19]

By now the family dispute we have been examining had become quite localised, and other issues were coming to the fore, notably biblical criticism, the Oxford Movement, evolutionary theory, and the like. But the question of the nature and relations of God and man had not been solved; it had only been shelved. From time to time Arminianism was asserted, as by the Methodist theologian W. B. Pope (1822–1903).[20] Calvinism was stoutly defended by the Baptist C. H. Spurgeon (1834–92).[21] But that the *debate* was more or less over was indicated as clearly as by anything else by the fact that in 1891, after many vicissitudes, the traditionally Calvinistic Baptist Union could merge with the evangelical Arminians of the New Connexion.[22] Whilst we should not wish to express ourselves in exactly the same terms as John Gill:

> 'I should be glad to see the Pelagian and Arminian controversies set on foot . . . for whatever the charitable men of our age may suggest to the contrary, controversies are as usual to the churches . . . as winds are to purify the air, purge the waters, and, by that means, prevent pestilential distempers'[23]

— we nevertheless feel that an intense concern for doctrinal clarity, provided it could be fostered without acrimony, would be a refreshing change from that neutralism and relativism into which so much recent theology has fallen. Our feeling concerning our times is remarkably similar to that of Principal D. W. Simon (1830–1909) concerning his. Addressing the International Congregational Council in 1891 he said,

> 'In 1871 an American correspondent of the Boston *Congregationalist* wrote: "In England there has been so little doctrinal preaching or theological teaching for the last forty years that the congregations have very little idea of the completeness or strength of the Calvinistic argument." Now, one might say, they have no idea at all! What used, however, to be lack of interest has largely deepened into positive dislike, not to say contempt. When prominent ministers refer in tones of mock humility to their ignorance of Systematic Theology, or earn cheap applause by denouncing dogma and contrasting it with life . . . when it is easier to get a thousand pounds to build a college than a hundred to provide adequate teaching — what else can one

say? . . . During the last thirty-five years only one "Systematic Theology" has been published by British Congregationalists . . . out of some 600 registered Congregational publications during, say, twenty-five years, scarcely 50 are scientifically theological . . . out of upwards of 450 discourses by Congregational ministers printed during the last five years or thereabouts in *The Christian World Pulpit,* scarcely thirty were properly doctrinal.'[24]

In his remarks Dr. Simon encompassed the whole field of doctrine, and he went on to qualify his remarks as far as inspiration, the atonement and future punishment were concerned; but for a specific comment upon the debate with which we have been chiefly concerned, we may turn to R. W. Dale who, in a speech delivered in November 1876, remarked upon the 'obvious' fact of 'the general disappearance of Calvinism' from contemporary theological thought.[25] It therefore comes as no surprise that by 1908 Dr. Robert Mackintosh could write of the Calvinist-Arminian debate that 'The controversy has gone to sleep. Or judgment in the case goes by default'.[26] We quite understand that the strenuous effort of debate can momentarily exhaust, and that other concerns can and do become fashionable; but the fact that both of Mackintosh's sentences were *and remain* true[27] is not, given the centrality of the old issues to the Christian message, an altogether happy indication of theological seriousness.

We confess, in conclusion, that by being as single-minded as possible in tracing our family dispute over the God-man relation we have been guilty of a certain artificiality. We have proceeded almost as if the broader intellectual environment did not influence doctrine. In fact, of course, it did. Again, with certain exceptions, our work has been limited geographically to Britain. It would have been quite possible, for example, to have traced the nineteenth-century slackening of grip upon things Calvinistic in Holland, America and elsewhere. Such limitations notwithstanding, we offer our tentative findings.

However variously the points at issue were expressed, the underlying questions were these: What is the nature of man's plight, and who is competent to rescue him from it? How may man be right with God? Whence comes the redemptive initiative? How far, if at all, is man able to co-operate with God in the matter of his own salvation? Few put the issues so bluntly, or gave his own answer more clearly, than the Italian Reformer Jerome Zanchius (1516–90):

> 'Conversion and salvation must, in the very nature of things, be wrought and effected either by ourselves alone, or by ourselves and God together, or *solely by God Himself.* The Pelagians were for the first. The Arminians are for the second. True believers are for the last, because the last hypothesis, and that only, is built on the strongest evidence of Scripture, reason and experience: it most effectually hides pride from man, and sets the crown of undivided praise upon the head, or rather casts it at the feet, of that glorious *Triune God,* who worketh all in all.'[28]

We have seen how this judgment has been endorsed by Calvinists of succeeding centuries, and in our own day we can find Professor John Murray declaring that the denial of unconditional election 'means that the determining factor in salvation is what man himself does, and that is just tantamount to saying that it is not God who determines the salvation of men, but men determine their own salvation; it is not God who saves but man saves himself. This is precisely the issue'.[29] Similarly, John R. de Witt has averred that 'Arminianism essentially represents an attack upon the majesty of God; and puts in place of it, the exaltation of man'.[30] But no one saw more clearly than Robert Mackintosh, himself a refugee (to use his own term) from Calvinism, the dangers on both sides of the question: 'The God of the Calvinist, who deliberately foreordains His creatures to eternal sin and eternal misery, is certainly morally incredible. But the God of the evangelical Arminian, whose will is divided against His own nature, — who does His utmost to redeem the human race, and reluctantly sees men (in spite of God's utmost) going on to a certain eternity of sin and misery — such a God is intellectually hard to conceive.'[31]

After we have taken account of the fact that we may not draw a straight line from Pelagius to Wesley, or from Augustine to Whitefield, Gill or Gadsby; when we have observed that in important respects Arminius was not an Arminian; when we have paid due attention to the Wesley's *intention* (however inconsistently realised) to ascribe all the glory of salvation to God; and having allowed for the fact that Calvin would have rested uneasily with some later Calvinists, and that whilst a few defended, still fewer practised, antinomianism — after all the qualifications have been made, we are left with a real and crucial divide within Christian theology. On the one hand, the ethical protest of Pelagius, and the Arminian denunciation of the more crippling forms of Calvinism must ever be accorded due weight. If ever those in the Augustinian-Calvinist line disjoin God's justice and power from his love and mercy in such a way that the former become capricious and arbitrary, then a swift return to the scriptures must be made in order to restore to its rightful place the doctrine of God-*in-Christ*. (There is nothing so effective as those last two words in challenging the incipient deism of the 'orthodox'). Again, if Calvinists should ever so denigrate man to the extent of removing from his free agency, or the *obligation* to repent and believe (these being genuinely man's own acts, yet possible only because of God's logically prior, if not always temporally distinct, act of regeneration), then, once more, they need to return to the scriptures. On the other hand, when reading the work of those who stand (for all their important individual differences) in the Arminian line, it is all too easy to feel that they have paid insufficient attention to the Anselmian retort, 'Thou has not yet considered the gravity of sin'. It is because it is more realistic in face of that challenge that our own preference at this point is for an ameliorated Calvinism. And, to end as we began with 'Rabbi' Duncan: among the marks of an ameliorated Calvinism is that it enunciates this truth that 'There is a true and a false synergia. That God works half, and man the other half, is false; that God works all, and man does all, is true'.[32]

Glossary

The use of a number of technical terms in the text was unavoidable. Such terms are convenient shorthand, but they are often notoriously slippery. This is especially so when they have been used as party labels (or weapons). We take the risk that nutshell definitions may obscure more than they reveal, in the hope of assisting the general reader through the theological thickets we have undertaken to explore. In offering our definitions we have in mind the way in which the several terms were used in the classical debates, and not those refinements of some of them which have more recently been suggested. The terms 'Arminianism' and 'Calvinism' are discussed in the text, and do not appear here.

Amyraldism (from Moise Amyraut, 1596–1664): the view that the atonement, though universal in its scope and therefore in harmony with God's antecedent decree of salvation, is effectual only in the case of the elect.

Antinomianism: the view that since Christ both bore the penalty of sin and fulfilled the law, those under grace are not required to obey the moral law.

Creationism: the doctrine that a new soul is created every time a new human being is conceived or born. (See 'Traducianism')

Decree, The Divine: the eternal, comprehensive, unchangeable, efficacious plan of the triune God in respect of creation, providence and redemption. When for convenience the plural is used the ultimate reference is still to the one all-embracing plan of the sovereign God.

Election: the eternal, unchangeable, unconditional call of God, whereby some are saved and God is glorified. (See 'Predestination' and 'Reprobation')

Federal Theology: that theology which builds upon a covenant of works said to have been made between God and Adam (as representative head of the human race), and a covenant of grace between God and Christ (as Second Adam).

Governmentalism: the view of Grotius (1583–1645) to the effect that since God could invoke or relax the moral law at will, Christ was not so much our substitute, as the one who on grounds of 'administrative tidiness' honoured God's justice, thereby impressing man with sin's hideousness.

Imputation: the doctrine concerning the way in which men, as descendants of Adam, share his guilt. The doctrine of immediate imputation states that the guilt of man's representative, Adam, is immediately imputed (or accounted) to his descendants. The doctrine of mediate imputation states that Adam's guilt is communicated *via* natural generation — i.e. men are guilty because they are corrupt, and not *vice versa*. The perfect righteousness of Christ is imputed to the sinner in justification, and on this ground alone, and not because of his own faith, the sinner is accepted by God.

Infralapsarianism: the view that the decree of predestination presupposes the creation and fall of man. (See 'Predestination' and 'Supralapsarianism').

Neonomianism: the view that since the saved enjoy more of the Holy Spirit's grace than the unsaved, the former are competent as the latter are not to fulfil the new law of Christ.

Pelagianism (after Pelagius, born c. 370): the view that man is not totally unable to please God, and that he has it in him to discipline himself to God-pleasing ends, and to move towards God apart from enabling grace.

Perfectionism: the doctrine that perfection is attainable by believers in this present life; or (in weaker versions) that even if absolute perfection eludes the believer in this life, the quest of it is to be maintained.

Perseverance of the Saints: the doctrine that those whom God has regenerated and effectually called to himself cannot finally fall away from him, and cannot be other than eternally saved.

Pietism: a seventeenth-century reaction against theological aridity in the direction of an experimentalism which sometimes degenerated into mysticism on the one hand, or into a new legalism on the other.

Predestination: the doctrine concerning God's purpose for fallen men. He decrees that some shall be elected to salvation and (hence the term 'double predestination') that others shall be reprobate. The latter, being sinners, are passed by ('preterition') to the end that God's justice might be manifest. (See 'Election' and 'Reprobation').

Reprobation: the eternal, unchangeable, unconditional casting off by God of some sinners, in accordance with his decree. (See 'Election' and 'Predestination').

Sandemanianism (after Robert Sandeman, 1718–1771): the view that intellectual assent to the apostolic testimony concerning the work of Christ suffices for salvation, and that considerations respecting the hearer's will, emotions and obedience are beside the point.

Socinianism (after Faustus Socinus, 1539–1604): the doctrine that Christ was not essentially divine. Socinus was *a* father of later Unitarianism.

Supralapsarianism: the view that the decree of predestination includes the decrees to create man and to permit him to fall. (See 'Infralapsarianism').

Traducianism: the doctrine that the soul is generated with the body. (See 'Creationism').

Universalism: the doctrine that by the mercy of God all men shall at last be saved, albeit *via* the purgation of hell.

Notes

CHAPTER ONE

1. Ed. William Knight, *Colloquia Peripatetica . . . being notes of conversations with the late John Duncan,* 6th edn. Edinburgh and London: Oliphant 1907, p.29.

2. W. Cunningham, *The Reformers and the Theology of the Reformation* (1862), London: The Banner of Truth Trust 1967, pp.301—2.

3. A. M. Fairbairn, *The Place of Christ in Modern Theology,* London: Hodder and Stoughton 1894, p.144. How strangely refreshing and restful is such Victorian prose!

4. Fairbairn noted that the first edition of the *Institutes* (1536), though only a sketch, reveals that 'the emphasis lies less on dogma than on morals, worship, polity'. *Ibid.,* p.147. It is, moreover, true that the material in Calvin's polemical writings is necessarily determined by his antagonists. Failure to remember this may, once more, result in an unbalanced view of the main thrust of his work.

5. The making of this trite point blunts the edge of some caricatures of Calvin — and may surprise some latter day sabbatarian Calvinists.

6. On this last point see Robert D. Linder, 'Calvinism and Humanism: the First Generation', *Church History* XLIV 1975, pp.167—181.

7. Philip C. Holtrop, review of James Daane, *The Freedom of God,* Grand Rapids: Eerdmans 1974, in *Calvin Theological Journal* X 1975, p.214.

8. On the space accorded to predestination see Wilhelm Niesel, *The Theology of Calvin,* trans. Harold Knight, Philadelphia: Westminster Press 1956, pp.165—6.

9. Carl Bangs, *Arminius: A Study in the Dutch Reformation,* Nashville & New York: Abingdon Press 1971, p.66.

10. See I. John Hesselink, 'The Charismatic Movement and the Reformed Tradition', *Reformed Review* XXVIII 1975, pp.149—51. For all his appreciation of neo-Pentecostalism, Dr. Hesselink finds that at crucial points the Pentecostals are not Pentecostal *enough.* We hear little from them of the Spirit in creation; of the relation between Word and Spirit; or of the relations between the Spirit and the Church, the sacraments, tradition, and the Christian life. (p.155).

11. John T. McNeill, 'John Calvin : Doctor Ecclesiae' in ed. J. H. Bratt, *The Heritage of John Calvin*, Grand Rapids : Eerdmans 1973, p.11.

12. For illuminating statements on Calvin the man see F. Wendel, *Calvin*, London: Collins Fontana 1965, especially pp.37–45; T. H. L. Parker, *Portrait of Calvin*, London: S.C.M. 1954 and *John Calvin*, London: Dent 1975; P. E. Hughes, 'John Calvin: The Man Whom God Subdued', in *How Shall They Hear?* Puritan Papers London 1960, pp.5–10: O. R. Johnston, 'Calvin the Man' in *Able Ministers of the New Testament*, Puritan Papers London 1964, pp.19–35. This last volume contains articles on other aspects of Calvin's life and thought, by R. A. Finlayson, J. I. Packer, G. E. Duffield, W. J. Grier, and D. M. Lloyd-Jones.

13. W. Cunningham, *The Reformers . . .*, p.338.

14. A. M. Fairbairn, *op. cit.*, p.149.

15. Carl Bangs, 'Arminius as a Reformed Theologian', in ed. J. H. Bratt, *op. cit.*, pp.212, 213–4. For a fuller account see his book at n.10 above.

16. *Ibid.*, p.217, citing a letter to Hippolytus à Collibus dated 5.iv. 1608. Cf. *Works* II, pp.685–705.

17. G. F. Nuttall, 'The Influence of Arminianism in England' in *The Puritan Spirit*, London: Epworth 1967, p.78. Cf. H. Orton Wiley, *Christian Theology*, 3 vols. Kansas City: Beacon Hill Press, 1940–3. C. Bangs accepts Dr. Nuttall's characterisation of Arminianism as applying to Dutch and American Arminianism. See his 'Recent Studies in Arminianism', *Religion in Life* XXXII 1963, p.426. For our own treatment of the 'Arminians of the head' see A. P. F. Sell, 'Arminians, Deists and Reason', *Faith and Freedom* XXXIII Autumn 1979, pp.19–31.

18. J. Orr, *The Progress of Dogma*, London: James Clarke n.d. but preface has 1901, p.296. Orr points out that it was the milder, infralapsarian view which prevailed at Dort. According to this view God's electing grace interposed to save *already fallen* man. Cunningham declares that supralapsarianism 'has been held by comparatively few Calvinistic theologians', *The Reformers . . .*, p.359. But Fairbairn holds, without specifying them, that 'The greatest of the Reformed divines were supralapsarian'. *Op. cit.*, p.168 n.

19. See 'A Declaration of the Sentiments of Arminius', *Works* I, trans. James Nichols, London: Longmans 1925 –, pp.516–668. For the course of the controversy see A. W. Harrison, *Arminianism*, London: Duckworth, 1937.

20. *Op. cit.*, p.521.

21. *Ibid.*, p.553. In a note Nichols, Arminius's sympathetic translator,

comments: 'Such calumnious reproaches appear most pre-
posterously applied to the Arminians, whose tenets, from their
very origin, have always had a tendency to exalt the *grace of God*
to its scriptural elevation; while the doctrines of Calvin and his
imitators have seized on a solitary apostolic expression, (*O
wretched man that I am!*) to beat down the legitimate aspirings of
Divine Grace after a holy conformity to God, and to controvert
and explain away the positive commands of God our Saviour concerning personal sanctity.'

22. *Ibid.*, p.555.

23. *Ibid.*

24. *Ibid.*, p.559.

25. *Ibid., p.561.*

26. *Ibid.*, p.570.

27. *Ibid.*, p.575.

28. *Ibid.*, pp.589—90.

29. *Ibid.*, pp.595—6.

30. *Ibid.*, p.602.

31. Quoted by C. Bangs, *art. cit.*, p.218.

32. *Ibid.*

33. C. Bangs, *Arminius* . . ., p.354.

34. See his 'Apology or Defence . . . against Thirty-one Theological
Articles', *Works* II, p.9.

35. A. M. Fairbairn, *op. cit.*, p.171.

36. *Ibid.*

37. See D. N. Steele and C. C. Thomas, *The Five Points of Calvinism*,
Philadelphia: Presbyterian and Reformed 1963.

38. For Calvin's teaching on man see T. F. Torrance, *Calvin's Doctrine
of Man*, London: Lutterworth 1949. For general expositions of
Calvinism see the works cited of Cunningham, Wendel, Parker; see
also A. Dakin, *Calvinism*. London: Duckworth 1940; B. B. Warfield
Calvin and Augustine, Philadelphia : Presbyterian and Reformed,
1956.

39. J. Calvin, *Institutes of the Christian Religion*, 2 vols., ed. J. T.
McNeill, trans. Ford Lewis Battles, London: S.C.M. Press 1960, I
ii 1, iii 1, v 2.11.

40. *Ibid.*, II i 8. The Anglican William Cunningham seems to misinter-
pret 'total' in 'total depravity' in denying that Calvin follows
Augustine here. See *S. Austin and His Place in the History of
Christian Thought*, London: Clay 1886, p.83. Robert Mackintosh,
a self-confessed refugee from Calvinism, wrote: 'Calvinism used to

pretend that the heathen had light enough to condemn but not to save; to which one's conscience replied that the only ground why light condemns is that, if better employed, it might save.' *Christianity and Sin*, London: Duckworth 1913, p.86. For the life and thought of Mackintosh see A. P. F. Sell, *Robert Mackintosh: Theologian of Integrity*. Bern: Peter Lang, 1977.

41. J. Calvin, *Concerning the Eternal Predestination of God*, trans. J. K. S. Reid, London: James Clarke 1961, VIII 5. The reference is to Augustine's *Enchiridion ad Laur.* 99. Cf. *Institutes* III xxiii 8.

42. *Institutes* I xviii 4. Cf. I xvii 11, where Satan is similarly used by God.

43. W. Cunningham, *Historical Theology* (1862) reprinted London: The Banner of Truth Trust 1960, II, p.389.

44. W. Cunningham, *The Reformers . . .*, p.339.

45. *Institutes*, II iii 5.

46. *Ibid.*

47. *Ibid.*, II iii 4.

48. *Ibid.*, II ii 7.

49. F. Townley Lord, 'A Modern Estimate of Calvinism', *The Baptist Quarterly* IV 1928–9, p.86.

50. *Institutes*, II iii 6.

51. See his chapter 'Calvinism and the Doctrine of Philosophical Necessity' in *The Reformers . . .*, pp.471–524.

52. *Ibid.*, p.498. Cf. his *Historical Theology* I, pp.574, 578 and notes.

53. W. Cunningham the Anglican, *op. cit.*, pp.85–6, citing *Institutes*, II iv 3.

54. B. B. Warfield, *Calvin and Augustine*, p.294.

55. *Institutes*, III xxi i.

56. *Ibid.*, III xxi 7. For a classical Arminian statement on predestination see Peter Baro in Arminius's *Works* I, pp.92–100. From many Calvinist Statements we select B. B. Warfield on 'Predestination' in his *Biblical and Theological Studies*, Philadelphia: Presbyterian and Reformed 1952, pp.270–333.

57. *Concerning the Eternal Predestination of God*, p.156.

58. *Institutes*, III xxii 11. On this point Augustine was not as bold as Calvin: 'In his resolute denial that character and life had anything to do with determining the decrees of God, Calvin went farther than his master Augustine, who in his anti-Pelagian treatise suggests his inclination to a contrary opinion, conjecturing that in the case of those whom God gives over to evil some ill-deserts of

their own must have first occurred, so that they are justly requited with delinquency and obduracy.' A. Mitchell Hunter, The *Teaching of Calvin*, Glasgow: Maclehose 1920, pp.103—4.

59. W. Cunningham, *Historical Theology* II, p.426.

60. *Ibid.*, p.437—8.

61. *Concerning the Eternal Predestination of God*, p.157.

62. *Institutes*, II iii 11.

63. A. Moore, *Science and the Faith*, p.119. Cited by O. Hardman, *The Christian Doctrine of Grace*, London: Unicorn Press 1937, p.70.

64. J. S. Whale, *The Protestant Tradition*, Cambridge: C.U.P. 1960, p.143. Of A. Dakin, *op. cit., p.97.*

65. A. M. Fairbairn, *op. cit.*, pp.164—5. N. P. Williams reiterates Fairbairn's point with acknowledgements and approval, *The Grace of God*, London: Longmans 1930. p.6.

66. B. B. Warfield, *Calvin and Augustine*, pp.157—8. Warfield also rebukes D. W. Simon, *Reconciliation by Incarnation* (1898), p.282, for understanding 'Providential government of the world' to mean 'Pantheism'. *Op. cit.*, p.156, n.48.

67. *Concerning the Eternal Predestination of God*, VIII 6.

68. *Ibid.*, Introduction, p.40. Cf. T. H. L. Parker, *op. cit.*, pp.57—8. But contrast F. Wendel, *op. cit.*, p.231, where Calvin is interpreted as holding that 'The Christ took part in the election, because he is one of the three Persons of the Holy Trinity'.

69. J. Orr, *op. cit.*, pp.292, 294—5.

70. W. Ames, *De Conscientia* IV iv 9.4. This 1632 work is quoted by J. I. Packer, 'Arminianisms' in *The Manifold Grace of God*, Puritan and Reformed Studies Conference, London 1968, p.31. For a detailed account of Puritan theology on this point, on Antinomianism, etc., see Ernest F. Kevan, *The Grace of Law*, London: Carey Kingsgate 1964.

CHAPTER TWO

1. For Knox see *D.N.B.* XI, pp.308—328; Thomas McCrie, *Life of John Knox*, Edinburgh: 1845; Geddes MacGregor, *The Thundering Scot*, London Macmillan 1958; Gordon Donaldson, *The Scottish Reformation*, Cambridge: C.U.P. 1960; James S. E. McEwen, *The Faith of John Knox*, London: Lutterworth Press 1961; W. Stanford Reid, *Trumpeter of God*, New York: Scribners, 1974; ed. Duncan Shaw, *John Knox*, Edinburgh: The Saint Andrew Press 1975.

2. Donald Maclean, *Aspects of Scottish Church History*, Edinburgh: T. & T. Clark 1927, p.20.

3. *Scots Confesion* XII; we quote from ed. Arthur C. Cochrane, *Reformed Confesions of the 16th Century*, Philadelphia: Westminster Press 1966, pp.171—2.

4. See John Macleod, *Scottish Theology in Relation to Church History since the Reformation*, Edinburgh: Free Church of Scotland 1943, p.57. Reprinted by The Banner of Truth Trust 1974.

5. See his *Apologia Ecclesiae Anglicanae*, 1562, various translations.

6. See W. T. Whitley, *Calvinism and Evangelism in England especially in Baptist Circles*, London Kingsgate Press 1933, p.8.

7. A. M. Fairbairn, *Christ in Modern Theology*, London: Hodder & Stoughton 1894, p.183. Cf. N. P. Williams, *The Grace of God*, London: Longmans 1930, p.93, where the author notes the fact of the association of High Churchism with Arminianism, but does not adduce Fairbairn's reason for it. All the Calvinists and Arminians mentioned in the paragraph enjoy entries in *D.N.B.*

8. See J. Smyth's, *Works*, Cambridge: C.U.P. 1915, II pp.682, 738. For Smyth see W. H. Burgess, *John Smith, the Se-Baptist*, London: James Clarke 1911; *D.N.B.* XVIII, pp.476—8; and such general Baptist histories as W. T. Whitley, *A History of British Baptists*, London: Griffin 1923, and A. C. Underwood, *A History of the English Baptists*, London: Baptist Union 1947.

9. For this and other Baptist confessions see W. J. McGlothin, *Baptist Confessions of Faith*, London: Kingsgate Press n.d. but preface has 1910.

10. For Helwys see W. H. Burgess, *op. cit.; D.N.B.* IX, pp.375—6; general Baptist histories.

11. For Goodwin see Walter Wilson, *The History and Antiquities of Dissenting Churches and Meeting Houses in London, &c.*, II 1808, pp.403—425; Thomas Jackson, *The Life of John Goodwin*, London 1822, W. W. Biggs, *John Goodwin*, London: Independent Press, 1961. For his part A. M. Toplady rejoiced to quote Strype on the presence of free-willers in Kent and Essex in 1550 — ten years before Arminius was born. See Toplady's *Works*, London: Chidley 1837, p.59.

12. W. Wilson, *op. cit.*, p.416.

13. *Ibid.*, p.403.

14. *Ibid.*, p.408. Bp. Burnet accused Goodwin of millenarianism. Wilson thinks it unlikely that the accusation was just, since surely Edwards would not have overlooked such a 'sin'! *Ibid.*, p.417. No doubt a large part of the explanation of the acrimony which marred some of the debates of the time is that those who ardently be-

lieved in the authority of scripture sometimes found it hard not to believe as ardently in their logical deductions from it.

15. *Ibid.*, pp.410–11.

16. From Goodwin's *The Banner of Justification,* quoted by James Nichols, *The Works of James Arminius,* London, 1825, I p.xxii. Contemporaneously with the events just described (i.e. c. 1646) Hugh Evans of Llan-hir, aided by Jeremiah Ives of the Old Jewry congregation, London, founded a Welsh Arminian Baptist movement 'which insisted that God wills that all men should be saved and insisted equally firmly on close communion'. So W. T. Pennar Davies, 'Episodes in the History of Brecknockshire Dissent', *Brycheiniog* III 1957, p.14. Nor should it be forgotten that the seventeenth century Quakers likewise tended towards an Arminian-universalist position. Thus e.g.: 'this light [i.e. Christ] enlighteneth the hearts of all in a day, in order to salvation, *if it be not resisted:* nor is it less universal than the seed of sin . . .' Robert Barclay (1648–90), *An Apology for the True Christian Divinity* (Latin 1676; 1st English edn. 1678) 14th edn. Glasgow 1886, p.3 (our italics); cf. *ibid.*, pp.76–138.

17. Christopher Ness, *An Antidote Against Arminianism* (1700), London: Sovereign Grace Union 1920, p.2. For Ness (1621–1705) see A. W. Light, *Bunhill Fields II,* London: Farncombe 1933, pp.68–70.

18. See E. Coles, *A Practical Discourse of God's Sovereignity,* ed. Charles Stuart Sandford, Dublin: Herbert 1855; and a more recent reprint by the Sovereign Grace Union, London 1958. Coles, T. Goodwin and Annesley are in *D.N.B.*

19. Thomas Watson, *A Body of Divinity* (first published as part of *a Body of Practical Divinity,* (1692), revised edn. London: The Banner of Truth Trust 1965, p.285.

20. For Cameron see J. MacLeod, *op. cit.,* pp.60–3. For Amyraut see e.g. T. M. Lindsay, 'Amyraldism'. *E.R.E.* I, pp.404–6; L. Proctor's unpublished doctoral dissertation, *The Theology of Moise Amyraut considered as a reaction against Seventeenth Century Calvinism,* University of Leeds, 1952; Brian G. Armstrong, *Calvinism and the Amyraut Heresy,* U. Wisconsin Press 1969; R. R. Nicole, *Moyse Amyraut (1596–1664) and the controversy of universal grace, first phase (1634–1637),* Ph.D. dissertation, Harvard University 1966.

21. See D. H. Kromminga, *The Christian Reformed Tradition,* Grand Rapids: Eerdmans, 1943, p.48.

22. For Baxter see E.R.E.; D.N.B.; C. E. Surman, *Richard Baxter,* London: Independent Press, 1961, G. F. Nuttall, *Richard Baxter,* London: Nelson 1965. For Baxter's theology see J. I. Packer, *The Redemption and Restoration of Man in the Thought of Richard*

Baxter, unpublished doctoral dissertation, University of Oxford 1954. Amyraut's teaching confirmed Baxter in views he had attained by 1654, it did not originate his doctrinal stance. Among others whose views more or less coincided with Amyraut's were John Davenant (1570–1641), Edmund Calamy (1600–1666), and Edward Williams (1750–1813) – for whom see below; and in Scotland, James Fraser of Brea (1639–99), James Morison (1816–93) and Ralph Wardlaw (1779–1853), to all of whom further reference will be made. In addition to the continuing influence of Amyraldism on the continent, it may be noted that this type of thought found its way into the New England Theology, especially *via* Samuel Hopkins (1721–1803), whose success as an exponent of the *via media* may be judged by the fact that his position was denounced by some for being hyper-Calvinistic, and by others for being Arminian and Pelagian.

23.   Preface to *Certain Disputations,* 1658.

24.   Quoted by John McLachlan, *The Divine Image,* London: Lindsey Press 1972, p.143.

25.   J. Orr, *The Progress of Dogma,* London: James Clarke 1901, p.301. See also J. I. Packer, 'The Doctrine of Justification in Development and Decline among the Puritans', in *By Schisms Rent Asunder,* Puritan and Reformed Studies Conference, London 1969, pp.18–30. Of Baxter E. F. Kevan writes, 'Richard Baxter rejects the idea that the Law is eternal, and it is this which constitutes the fundamental difference between his teaching and that of most of his Puritan contemporaries'. *The Grace of Law,* p.67. Cf. J. I. Packer's dissertation, pp.303–5.

26.   For Rutherford see *D.N.B.* XVII, pp.496–8; A. Smellie, *Men of Covenant* (1903) London: The Banner of Truth Trust 1960, *passim;* ed. R. S. Wright, *Fathers of the Kirk,* London: O.U.P. 1960 pp.73–84.

27.   James Walker, *The Theology and Theologians of Scotland,* Edinburgh: T. & T. Clark, 1872, p.81.

28.   A. M. Fairbairn, *Christ in Modern Theology,* p.174 n.

29.   J. MacLeod, *op. cit.,* p.71. For Twisse see *D.N.B.* XIX, pp.1324–6.

30.   J. Walker, *op. cit.,* p.9.

31.   S. Rutherford, *The Trial and Triumph of Faith* (1645), Edinburgh 1845, pp.41–3.

32.   *Ibid.,* 'Dedication', p.10.

33.   Of this work Walker wrote, 'I need not say it is distinguished for brevity; but I have read it with more interest than I have been able to feel in some of the great English Puritans', *op. cit.,* p.22.

34.   For Traill see *D.N.B.* XIX, p.1077.

35. He wrote a letter, 'A vindication of the Protestant Doctrine con-
     cerning Justification . . . from the unjust Charge of Antinomianism'
     (1692). See R. Traill, *Works,* Edinburgh 1810, pp.252—296. The
     four vols. of Traill's *Works* have been reprinted by The Banner of
     Truth Trust, Edinburgh in 2 vols., 1975.

36. R. Traill, *Ibid.,* Ip.253. Traill wrote a memoir of his friend, the
     Evangelical Calvinist William Guthrie of Fenwick. So 'An Account
     of the Life and Character of the Author' prefixed to Traill's
     Works. pp.iv, vii. For a recent account of Guthrie see A. P. F. Sell,
     'The Christian's Great Interest — and the Preacher's', *The Evan-*
     gelical Quarterly, XLVI 1974, pp.72—80.

37. *Ibid.,* I, p.279.

38. See W. A. Brown, *The Essence of Christianity,* Edinburgh: T. & T.
     Clark, 1904, p.107. Cf. his article 'Covenant Theology' in *E.R.E.*
     IV, p.224a. Brown shows that Luther and Calvin knew only of
     the covenant of grace; likewise Bullinger in his 1534 work on the
     subject.

39. *Westminster Confession* VII. E. F. Kevan, *op. cit.,* p.111 gives some
     alternative names by which some Puritans knew the covenant of
     works.

40. Not least by A. H. Strong, *Systematic Theology* (1907) London:
     Pickering & Inglis 1956, p.612. For a recent discussion of the
     Westminster Confession see John H. Leigh, *Assembly at*
     Westminster, Richmond: John Knox Press 1973.

41. W. A. Brown refers us in this connection to Heppe's *Dogmatik des*
     deutschen Protestantismus im 16ten Jahrhundert, Gotha, 1857, I
     pp.143ff.

42. Dickson, Ames and Ball are in *D.N.B.* For Dickson see also
     J. MacLeod, *op. cit.,* pp.84—5.

43. J. Arminius, *Works* II, p.369.

44. *Ibid.,* pp.369—70.

45. *Ibid.,* 370.

46. R. Traill, *Works* I, p.277.

47. A. A. Hodge, *The Confession of Faith,* London: The Banner of
     Truth Trust 1958, p.125. Although we still await a definitive
     study of federal theology, the topic has recently come up for
     discussion — largely as a result of the publication of Holmes
     Rolston III, *John Calvin versus the Westminster Confession,*
     Richmond: John Knox Press, 1972. He maintains that the Confes-
     sion marks a serious departure from Calvin in that the concept of
     the law becomes dominant over that of grace, and this because of
     the federalist conceptual framework of the Confession. This
     argument is lucidly countered by Donald MacLeod, 'Federal
     Theology — an Oppressive Legalism?' *The Banner of Truth,* 125,

Feb. 1974, pp.21—8. He argues that the idea of the covenant of works is scriptural and that 'All the requirements of this idea are met by the promise of continuing communion with God' (p.22). Dr. Peter Toon (*Puritans and Calvinism*, Swengel, Penna.: Reiner, 1973, pp.60—1) seeks to maintain an intermediate position, to the effect that 'certain developments within the Reformed doctrinal tradition from 1560 to 1648 were departures from the teaching of Holy Scripture' (p.60). He makes three criticisms. We have already said enough to express our broad agreement with the second and third, namely, that predestination assumes a *potentially* (our word) unhealthily dominant position in the Confession, and that the sufficiency of the work of Christ is in danger (Dr. Toon is more positive) of subversion under the particularist view of election proposed in the Confession (though n.b. our remarks upon Rutherford). But the logic of his first criticism leaves something to be desired. He writes, 'As I see it, this system is too neat and tidy; it has everything wrapped up just a little too well; it stretches the Biblical data in favour of a systematic approach. Certainly the Bible has a lot to say about covenants but in that it took Reformed theologians several decades to work out this system it seems to me that it is just a little too good to be true' (p.60). Dr. Toon's claim in the first sentence here may or may not be true; without evidence it does not rise above the status of a prejudice. The second sentence is even more puzzling. Where, on this basis, would the doctrine of the Trinity be? The truth of doctrines is not necessarily related to their speed of formulation. We may note two further criticisms of federalism: (1) That the system reinforces what has been urged against Augustine, namely, that pre-Fall Adam was dealt with on *Pelagian* lines. But D. MacLeod has the answer to this: 'Paul in his polemic against legalism never argues that the idea, "Do this and live!" is intrinsically ungodly. It constitutes an impossible arrangement for man now, because of his spiritual inability. But in itself there is no absurdity in the idea that the man who fulfils the law shall live by it. Indeed, to say that the idea of merit is inherently inadmissible is to strike at the relation between God and Christ, which . . . was certainly one of meritorious obedience' (p.23). Mr. MacLeod enlists the aid of Robert Rollock; 'It could not well stand with the justice of God to make a covenant under condition of good works and perfect obedience to his law, except he had first created man pure and holy, and had engraven his law in his heart, whence those good works might proceed'. (P.24, quoting from Rollock's *Treatise on Effectual Calling*, in *Select Works* of Robert Rollock, 1849, I p.34). (2) That the unhistoricity of federalism threatens the significance of Christ. This criticism was discussed by W. Adams Brown, *The Essence of Christianity*, Edinburgh: T. & T. Clark, 1904, pp.107—111. He would agree with his contemporary J. Orr that the covenant theology 'brought the divine purpose into connection with time, and gave it something of that flexibility and movement — that *dynamical* character — which we have described as the corrective to the *static* conceptions of the eternal decree' (*Op. cit.*, p.303): Brown quotes Robertson Smith with approval: 'with all its defects . . . [it] is the most important attempt, in the older Protestant theology, to do justice to the historical development of revelation.' (E.R.E. *art. cit.*, p.218b, quoting Smith's *Prophets of Israel*, Edinburgh 1882, p.375). Brown still felt, however, that Christ's originality 'if not denied, is at least seriously minimized' by the federal theology (p.108). See also G. Thomas, 'Covenant theology — a historical survey' in *On Becoming a Christian*, London: Westminster Conference 1972, pp.5—21; J. B. Torrance, 'The contribution of McLeod Campbell to Scottish theology', *The Scottish Journal of Theology* XXIV, 1973, pp.295—311; M. Eugene Osterhaven, 'Calvin on the Covenant,' *Reformed Review* XXXIII 1980, pp.136—149.

48. P. Toon, *op. cit.*, chap. V.

49. *Ibid.*, p.80, comparing Chapter XV i and ii of each Confession.

50. *Ibid.*, p.81 (our italics).

51. It is strange that Dr. Toon should go on to say that 'The reasons for the writing and inclusion of this chapter [i.e. the new chapter XX] are not wholly clear since no minutes or records of the Savoy Assembly are extant' (p.81). He surmises that the question of the propagation of the gospel and the need, over against sectaries, to distinguish the true from the false gospel were operative factors. These may indeed be remote causes. But we need look no further than the Preface to the *Declaration* itself to find the proximate cause. There the divines explain that 'After the 19th *cap. of the Law*, we have added a *cap. of the Gospel*, it being a Title that may not well be omitted in a Confession of Faith; In which Chapter, what is dispersed, and by imitation in the Assemblies Confession with some little addition, is brought here together, and more fully under one head'. See ed. A. G. Matthews, *The Savoy Declaration of Faith and Order*, London: Independent Press, 1959, p.67.

52. W. T. Whitley, *Calvinism and Evangelism*, p.10. As Whitley explains, with reference to Roger Williams, John Eliot, *et al.*, 'This was based on actual doings in New England'.

53. P. Toon, *op. cit.*, p.83.

54. P. Toon, *God's Statesman: The Life and Work of John Owen*, Exeter: Paternoster Press, 1971, p.170. For Owen see also *D.N.B.* and A. W. Light *op. cit.* I, 1913, pp.84—92.

55. G. P. Fisher, *A History of Christian Doctrine*, Edinburgh: T. & T. Clark, p.348. Fisher properly points out (p.350) that the theory of Owen and his contemporaries is the Augustino-Federal theory

of the problem of imputation. That is, it is realistic and federal. In later federal theology the realism was largely dropped, owing to the long-standing difficulty of reconciling the idea of a generic sin in Adam with creationism.

56. W. A. Brown, *E.R.E. art. cit.*, pp.223—4.

57. A selection of his letters (first published in 1664), many of which are on these themes, has been published by The Banner of Truth Trust, 1973.

58. From Mason's *Select Remains*, 1970's reprint (n.d.) under the title *Mason's Sayings*, Sheffield: Zoar Publications, p.14.

59. P. Toon describes his conversion under a substitute country preacher in *God's Statesman*, p.13.

60. J. Owen, *The Death of Death in the Death of Christ*, ed. J. I. Packer, London: The Banner of Truth Trust, 1963, p.47. In his *Display of Arminianism* Owen asserted the view that Christ's death was sufficient for the whole world, but effective only for the elect. At this point he went further in explanation than did Calvin (cf. our remarks above on Calvin's alleged logical rigour). Owen thus placed himself in the line of Alexander of Hales, and on a par with the Synod of Dort and with Reformed confessionalism generally. See T. F. Torrance, 'Reformed Dogmatics not Dogmatism', *Theology* LXX, 1967, p.156.

61. See R. Baxter's appendix to *Aphorisms of Justification* (1640), and Owen's rejoinder, *Of the Death of Christ, the Price He paid* ... London: 1650. Isaac Chauncy (1632—1712) defended Owen in *A Theological Dialogue, containing a Defence and Justification of Dr. John Owen from the forty-two errors charged upon him by Mr. Richard Baxter*, 1684, and *the Second Part of the Theological Dialogue, being a rejoinder to Mr. Richard Baxter, 1684.*

62. *Romans*, iii, 8, 31.

63. J. MacBride Sterrett, 'Antinomianism', *E.R.E.* I, p.582a, citing Luther's *Werke* XX, p.203, and Melanchthon's *Loci Communes*, 1st edn. by Augusti, p.127.

64. *Ibid.*, but no reference given. Sterrett's account of later antinomianism is sketchy in the extreme. He mentions only Saltmarsh, Wesley and Fletcher by name — all within nine lines — and is completely silent on the American controversy.

65. *Institutes* II, vii, 13.

66. The literature is considerable, and the interpretations varied. See e.g. Perry Miller, *The New England Mind: II From Colony to Province*, (1953) Boston: Beacon Press, 1961, chapter IV: Larzer Ziff, *The Career of John Cotton*, Princeton: Princeton U.P., 1962: Norman Pettitt, *The Heart Prepared: Grace and Conversion in Puritan Spiritual Life*, New Haven & London: Yale U.P., 1966;

David D. Hall, *The Antinomian Controversy 1636–1638*, Middletown: Wesleyan U.P., 1968; and *The Faithful Shepherd: A History of New England Ministry in the Seventeenth Century*, Chapel Hill: U. of North Carolina Press, 1972: James W. Jones, *The Shattered Synthesis*, New Haven & London: Yale U.P., 1973, chapter I. The following are among the briefer studies: Edmund Morgan, 'The case against Ann Hutchinson', *New England Quarterly*, X, 1937, pp.635–649; K. M. Campbell, 'The Antinomian Controversies of the Seventeenth Century' in *Living the Christian Life*, London: The Westminster Conference 1974, pp.61–81 (this paper outlines the English controversies as well); William K. B. Stoever, 'Nature Grace and John Cotton', *Church History*, XLIV, 1975, pp.22–33.

67. Ed. Perry Miller, *The American Puritans*, New York: Anchor Books, 1956, p.50.

68. *Ibid.*, pp.49–50.

69. *Ibid.*, pp.53–4.

70. W. K. B. Stoever, *art. cit.*, p.26.

71. G. F. Nuttall, 'Calvinism in Free Church History', *The Baptist Quarterly*, XXII, 1968, p.425. Cf. J. MacLeod, op. cit., p.136.

72. See R. Thomas, *Daniel Williams 'Presbyterian Bishop'*, 1964, pp.12–14.

73. See F. Overend, *History of Ebenezer Baptist Church, Bacup*, London: Kingsgate, 1912; H. Wheeler Robinson, *The Life and Faith of the Baptists*, London: Methuen, 1927, p.46; Garth A. Weston, *The Baptists of North-West England, 1750–1850*, unpublished doctoral thesis, University of Sheffield, 1969, p.24.

74. W. T. Whitley, *A History of the British Baptists*, p.306.

75. L. E. Elliott-Binns, *Religion in the Victorian Era*, London: Lutterworth Press, 1936, p.54. This point is made by Dr. Weston, *op. cit.*

76. J. Buchanan, *The Doctrine of Justification* (1867), London: The Banner of Truth Trust, 1961, p.175.

77. Robert Traill claimed not to know any London minister or Christian who corresponded to the description of the antinomian vilifiers. See his *Works* I, p.281. Dr. Kevan reminds us that in his *Gangraena* Thomas Edwards charged the antinomians with one hundred and seventy six errors 'ranging from a denial of the Trinity to eating black puddings'. *Op. cit.*, p.33, n.116.

78. For Crisp see *D.N.B.*, V, pp.99–100.

79. R. Thomas, 'Parties in Nonconformity' in G. Bolam *et al.*, *The English Presbyterians*, London: Allen and Unwin, 1968, p.107.

80. J. I. Packer, 'The Doctrine of Justification . . .' *op. cit.*, p.30, n.14.

81.   See *D.N.B., art. cit.*

82.   Ed. John Gill, *Christ Alone Exalted . . . being the Complete Works of Tobias Crisp*, London, Bennett, 1832, II, p. 171, in Sermon XXXIV on *I John*, ii, 1, 2, 'Revelation of grace, no encouragement to sin'.

83.   S. Rutherford, *The Trial and Triumph of Faith*, sermon XVI, p.175.

84.   In Sermon V on *Col.*, i 18, 'Christ's Pre-eminence', I, p.78.

85.   *Westminster Confession*, XI, 4.

86.   T. Crisp, *Works* I, p.283.

87.   See his *The Honeycombe of Free Justification*, 1642. For Eaton see *D.N.B.* VI, pp.336—7. Other antinomian writers included John Saltmarsh (d.1647), William Dell and Henry Denne. Their opponents included Thomas Gataker (1574—1654), Thomas Edwards and John Sedgwick.

88.   *Works* II, p.285; a second sermon on *Col.* i 18.

89.   Roger Thomas, *art. cit.*, p.107. The entire chapter is useful for the ecclesiastical implications of the debate. For the more strictly theological aspects see P. Toon, *Puritans and Calvinism*, chapter VI. Robert Traill ascribed the renewed debate to Baxterian neonomianism rather than to the republication of Crisp's book. See his *Works* I, p.252.

90.   See *D.N.B.* X, pp.85—88.

91.   See *D.N.B.* IV, p.730.

92.   T. Watson, *The Ten Commandments* (first published as part of a *Body of Practical Divinity* 1692), London: The Banner of Truth Trust revised edn., 1965, p.44.

93.   For fuller details of the issues and events summarised in this paragraph see R. Tudur Jones, *Congregationalism in England;* London: Independant Press, 1962, pp.114—117; R. Thomas *art: cit.;* P. Toon, *Puritans and Calvinism*, pp.89—93; and especially G. F. Nuttall, 'Northamptonshire and *The Modern Question:* a Turning-Point in Eighteenth-Century Dissent', *The Journal of Theological Studies*, NS XVI, 1965, pp.101—123. Chauncy and Williams are in *D.N.B.* Williams is in A. W. Light, *op. cit.* II, pp.103—6.

94.   David Bogue and James Bennett, *History of Dissenters*, I, 1808, p.407.

95.   *Ibid.*, IV, 1812, pp.392—4.

96.   *Ibid.*, I, pp.405—6.

97.   *Ibid.*, p.418.

98. Hussey is not in *D.N.B.* G. F. Nuttall refers to him (*art.* n.93 above, pp. 111–114); and in his 'Cambridge Nonconformity 1660– 1710: from Holcroft to Hussey', *The Journal of the United Reformed Church History Society*, I, 9, 1977. pp.241–258. See also, Robert E. Seymour, *John Gill, Baptist Theologian (1697– 1771)* unpublished doctoral thesis, University of Edinburgh, 1954, pp.51–4. A large part of Hussey's *God's Operations of Grace but no offers of Grace* (1707) has recently been republished by Primitive Publications, Elon College, N.C., n.d. but preface has 1973. Our quotations are from this edition.

99. G. F. Nuttall, 'Northamptonshire and *The Modern Question . . .*', p.112, citing the Cambridge Church Book, printed in A. G. Matthews, *Diary of a Cambridge Minister*, Cambridge: Driver, 1937. One of the most fascinating aspects of English free church history is the link between doctrine and churchmanship. Thus, whereas such a church as that at Kendal began Presbyterian and became Unitarian, thereby changing its denomination consequent upon its doctrinal shift, the church at Carlton changed its denomination because it sought *no* doctrinal charge; and thus while all around has changed, it has ever remained Calvinist and has been, in turn, Congregational and Baptist, and is now Strict Baptist. For the Carlton illustration, and for other reflections on the theme see G. F. Nuttall, 'Calvinism in Free Church History'.

100. J. Hussey, *God's Operations of Grace*, pp.21, 23.

101. *Ibid.*, pp.31, 32, 34, 35, 37.

102. *Ibid.*, p.55.

103. *Ibid.*, p.110.

104. *Ibid.*, p.154.

105. *Ibid.*, p.159.

106. J. MacLeod, *op. cit.*, p.141. We may contrast Hussey's spirit with that of his older contemporary, Robert Traill: 'If there be any price or money spoke of [i.e. in connection with the gospel offer], it is *no price, no money.* And where such are the terms and conditions if we be forced to call them so, we must say, that they look like a renouncing, than a boasting of any qualifications or conditions. Surely the terms of the Gospel-bargain are, God's free giving and our free taking and receiving.' *Works* I, p.277.

107. For the Marrow Controversy see e.g. J. MacLeod *op. cit.*; J. Walker, *op. cit.*, John McKerrow, *History of the Secession Church*, Edinburgh: Fullerton, 1847; Henry F. Henderson, *The Religious Controversies of Scotland*, Edinburgh: T. & T. Clark, 1905; Donald MacLean, *op. cit.*: J. H. S. Burleigh, *A Church History of Scotland*, London: O.U.P., 1960, pp.288–91; for a recent brief account of Boston (also in *D.N.B.*) see D. J. Innes, 'Thomas Boston of

Ettrick', in *Faith and a Good Conscience*, London: Puritan and Reformed Studies Conference 1963, pp.32—46. For the text itself see ed. C. G. McCrie, *The Marrow of Modern Divinity*, Glasgow, 1902. The classic account of Boston is ed. George D. Low. *A General Account of my life by Thomas Boston*, London: Hodder & Stoughton, 1908. See also Stewart Mechie, 'The Theological Climate in Early Eighteenth Century Scotland', in ed. Duncan Shaw, *Reformation and Revolution*, Edinburgh: The Saint Andrew Press, 1967.

108. Some, including Professor Burleigh (*op. cit.*, p.288) have attributed the work to Edward Fisher (fl. 1627—56) of Oxford, for whom see *D.N.B.* VI, pp.56—7. Others have ascribed the work to an illiterate barber. In the 'Dedication' to John Warner, Lord Mayor or London, the author describes himself as a 'poore inhabitant' of that city.

109. See J. Walker, *op. cit.*, and J. MacLeod, *op. cit.;* Alexander Whyte, *James Fraser, Laird of Brea*, Edinburgh: Oliphant, 1911; Duncan Fraser, *James Fraser of Brea: his life and writings, with special reference to his theory of universal redemption and its influence on religious thought in Scotland*, unpublished doctoral dissertation, University of Edinburgh, 1944.

110. L. B. Short, 'The Challenge to Scottish Calvinism', *The Hibbert Journal* LXII, 1963—4, p.89.

111. J. MacLeod, *op. cit.*, p.175.

112. E.g. in his *Memoirs*, Edinburgh, 1899.

113. Quoted by D. J. Innes, *art. cit.*, p.42.

114. Quoted by H. F. Henderson, *op. cit.*, p.24.

115. James Hadow and James Hog are in *D.N.B.*

116. J. MacLeod, *op. cit.*, p.144.

117. *The Marrow*, p.114.

118. It is interesting to note that in the concurrent debate over the liberal views of Professor Simson, Hadow and his supporters and the Marrowmen found themselves on the *same* side.

119. J. Macleod, *op. cit.*, p.162.

120. J. Walker, *op. cit.*, p.60.

CHAPTER THREE

1. For Maurice see Thomas Rees, *History of Protestant Nonconformity in Wales*, London: Snow, 1883, pp.302—5. G. F. Nuttall, 'Northamptonshire and *The Modern Question*', pp.108—10. Of

antinomian and legalist extremists Maurice wrote, 'Though they were like Sampson's Foxes, Tail to Tail, having different views, they had Firebrands fix'd to 'em.' Quoted by Elvet Lewis, *Nonconformity in Wales*, London: National Council of Evangelical Free Churches, 1904, p.61.

2. G. F. Nuttall, 'Northamptonshire and *The Modern Question*', pp.108—9.

3. Rowland and Harris are in *D.N.B.* For the Welsh situation see the two classics, Thomas Rees, *History of Protestant Nonconformity in Wales*, London: Snow, 1883; William Williams, *Welsh Calvinistic Methodism*, London: Presbyterian Church of England, 2nd edn. 1884. For more recent studies of Harris see G. F. Nuttall, *Howel Harris 1714—1773, The Last Enthusiast*, Cardiff U. Wales Press, 1965; Eifion Evans, *Howel Harris, Evangelist*, Cardiff: U. Wales Press, 1974; for Rowland see Hywel R. Jones, *Daniel Rowland, Man of Truth and Power*, Cardiff: Evangelical Library of Wales, 1971.

4. W. Williams, *op. cit.*, pp.31—2 George Whitefield was converted probably in April 1735; Harris dated his conversion at 25th May 1735, and his testimony is our authority for the approximate date of Rowland's conversion. Harris wrote that 'he was awakened about the same time as myself', M. H. Jones, *The Trevecca Letters*, Caernarvon: Calvinistic Methodist Book Agency, 1932, p.209. Easter 1735 saw the conversion of another leader of the revival, John Cennick (1717—55). Few with the slightest acquaintance with English church history can be unaware that the Wesleys were converted in May 1738. Whitefield (1714—70), John Wesley (1703 —91) and his brother Charles (1707—88) are in *D.N.B.* The literature on the Wesleys is enormous. For Whitefield see Luke Tyerman, *Life of Whitefield*, 2 vols. London, 1876; A. D. Belden, *George Whitefield*, London: Independent Press, 1961; A. Dallimore, *George Whitefield* I, London: The Banner of Truth Trust, 1970 — vol. 2 1980. For Griffith Jones see *D.N.B.* X, pp.991—992; David Jones *Life and Times of Griffith Jones, Sometime Rector of Llanddowror*, London: S.P.C.K., 1902.

5. Quoted by E. Evans, *op. cit.*, p.15.

6. *Ibid.*, p.16.

7. *Ibid.*, p.18.

8. Quoted by W. Williams, *op. cit.*, p.40.

9. H. Harris to John Lewis, 4th October 1740. *The Journal of the Historical Society of the Presbyterian Church of Wales*, LX, 1975, pp.45—7.

10. H. Harris to John Cennick, 27th October 1740, *The Journal H.S.P.C.W.*, LX, 1975, pp.48.

11. These are all in *D.N.B.* For other Anglican evangelicals see A. Skevington Wood, *Thomas Haweis, 1734—1820,* London: S.P.C.K.,

1957; G. C. B. Davies, *The Early Cornish Evangelicals, 1735–60*, London: S.P.C.K., 1951; G. R. Balleine, *History of the Evangelical Party in the Church of England* (1908), London: Church Book Room Press, new edn. 1951.

12. See Arthur P. Davis, *Isaac Watts, His Life and Works*, London: Independent Press, 1943, pp.51–2. Watts is in *D.N.B.* See also A. N. Light, *op. cit.* I, pp.241–7; E. Routley, *Isaac Watts*, London: Independent Press, 1961. In 1737 Watts and his Congregationalist colleague Dr. John Guyse (1680–1761) published Edwards's *A Faithful Narrative of the Surprizing Work of God in the Conversion of Many Hundred Souls in Northampton*. For this work see *The Works of Jonathan Edwards*, revised and ed. Edward Hickman (1834), London: The Banner of Truth Trust, I, pp.346–64. Doddridge is in *D.N.B.* See also ed. G. F. Nuttall, *Philip Doddridge, 1702–51, His Contribution to English Religion*, London: Indepen: dent Press, 1951. For Edwards see James Iverach, *Jonathan Edwards, A Biography*, Edinburgh, 1884; O. E. Winslow, *Jonathan Edwards, 1703–58*, New York, 1940; A. V. G. Allen, *Life and Writings of Jonathan Edwards*, Edinburgh, 1889; Perry Miller, *Jonathan Edwards*, New York: Sloane, 1949; P. Miller, *Errand into the Wilderness*, Cambridge Mass.: Harvard U.P., 1956; P. de Jong, *The Covenant Idea in New England Theology*, Grand Rapids: Eerdmans, 1945; Conrad Cherry, *The Theology of Jonathan Edwards: A Reappraisal*, Garden City, New York, 1966; James Carse, *Jonathan Edwards and the Visibility of God*, New York: Scribners, 1967; John Opie, *Jonathan Edwards and the Enlightenment*; Lexington: Heath, 1969; Harold Simonson, *Jonathan Edwards: Theologian of the Heart*, Grand Rapids: Eerdmans, 1974. For the influence of Edwards upon the English scene see E. A. Payne, *The Prayer Call of 1784*, 1941, and 'The Evangelical Revival and the Beginnings of the Modern Missionary Movement', *The Congregational Quarterly*, 1943, pp.223–236; D. Elwyn Edwards, *The Influence of Jonathan Edwards on the Religious Life of Britain in the XVIIIth Century and the First Half of the XIXth Century*, unpublished B. Litt. dissertation, University of Oxford, 1954; Olin G. Robison, *The Particular Baptists of England, 1760–1820*, unpublished doctoral dissertation, University of Oxford, 1963, pp.162–170.

13. See R. W. Dale, *History of English Congregationalism*, London: Hodder & Stoughton, 1907, pp.584–5. Dale quotes a letter written by Watts to Doddridge on 20th September 1743, and refers to J. D. Humphreys, *Correspondence of Doddridge*, 1829–31, IV, pp.269–70. G. F. Nuttall's *Calendar of the Correspondence of Philip Doddridge D.D.* is now to hand: London, H.M.S.O. 1979.

14. See A. G. Matthews, *Calamy Revised*, Oxford: O.U.P., 1934.

15. For Susanna (1669–1742) see John A. Newton, *Susanna Wesley*

and the Puritan Tradition in Methodism, London: Epworth, 1968. For Samuel (1662—1735) see Luke Tyerman, *The Life and Times of the Rev. Samuel Wesley,* 1866.

16. *The Arminian Magazine,* 1778, p.37.

17. G. F. Nuttall, *The Puritan Spirit,* London: Epworth Press, 1967, p.77. In the present paragraph we draw upon this work, pp.73—7, and upon A. W. Harrison, *Arminianism,* London: Duckworth, 1937, chapter VII. We should remember, however, that in the first edition of his *A Christian Library* Wesley confessed the worth of such Calvinist writers as T. Goodwin, Sibbes, Owen and others. See R. C. Monk, John Wesley, *His Puritan Heritage,* London: Epworth, 1967. Wesley also regarded John Goodwin highly, and published an abridgement of his 1642 work *Imputatio Fidei, or a Treatise of Justification.*

18. *Whitefield's Journals,* London: The Banner of Truth Trust, 1960, p.62. Edwin Sidney laid a false trail which some followed when he claimed that 'Whitefield was not a Calvinist until he went to America in 1739'. See his *The Life of Sir Richard Hill, Bart,* London: 1839, p.171.

19. *Ibid.*

20. *Ibid.,* p.335. Some have caused themselves unnecessary confusion by mistaking this J. Edwards for Jonathan. John Edwards (1637—1716) is in *D.N.B.*

21. Whitefield's letter is given in full in The Banner of Truth Trust edn. of his *Journals,* pp.571—588. Among others who replied to Wesley was Joseph Hart (see n.88 below). His work was entitled *The Unreasonableness of Religion, being remarks and adimadversions on Mr. John Wesley's Sermon on Romans xiii 32,* 1741. In it he drifted closer to antinomianism that he did in his hymns.

22. L. Tyerman, *The Life of the Rev. George Whitefield,* I, p.216.

23. *Whitefield's Journals,* p.287.

24. L. Tyerman, *The Life and Times of the Rev. John Wesley,* London, I, p.314. In view of the evidence just cited, we find ourselves in the unusual position of disagreeing with E. A. Payne who suggests that 'probably under the influence of Jonathan Edwards' Whitefield was a Calvinist. Doubtless he became a stronger Calvinist because of Edwards's influence. See E. A. Payne *The Free Church Tradition in the Life of England* (1944) London: Hodder, 1965, p.76. Some were even blunter in their assessment of the logical end of Arminianism. Thus e.g. Jonathan Warne wrote *Arminianism the Back-Door to Popery,* 1738. For a twentieth century equation of Arminian and Roman presuppositions see e.g. the many writings of Cornelius Van Til, and for his view in a nutshell see *The*

Intellectual Challenge of the Gospel, Philadelphia: Presbyterian and Reformed, 1953.

25.   With the details of the course of the controversy we are not concerned. These may be found in A. Dallimore, *op. cit.*, Tyerman, *op. cit.*; and are conveniently summarised by Abel Stevens. *The History of the Religious Movement of the Eighteenth Century called Methodism,* London, n.d., II, chapter III.

26.   *Whitefield's Journals,* p.62.

27.   George Eayrs in ed. W. J. Townsend *et al. A New History of Methodism,* London, Hodder & Stoughton 1909, I, pp.305—6.

28.   L. Tyerman, *The Life and Times of the Rev. John Wesley,* I, p.349. For a concise article on the doctrinal points at issue — and one which makes good use of primary sources, see Irwin W. Reist, 'John Wesley and George Whitefield: A Study in the Integrity of Two Theologies', *The Evangelical Quarterly,* XLVII, 1975, pp.26—40.

29.   For Hervey see *D.N.B.* IX, pp.733—5.

30.   For this dispute see E. Evans, *op. cit.*, chapter VI; William Williams, *op. cit.*, chapter X.

31.   T. Rees, *op. cit.*, p.385. Robert Sandeman (1718—71) so emphasised the sole sufficiency of faith as to provoke the charge of antinomianism. He is in *D.N.B.*

32.   *Minutes,* 1744, quoted by Tyerman, *The Life and Times of . . . Wesley,* III, pp.71—2.

33.   A. W. Harrison, *op. cit.*, p.203.

34.   For A. M. Toplady see *D.N.B.*; T. Wright, *The Life of Augustus M. Toplady,* London: Farncombe, 1911. We have used the 1837 edn. (reprinted verbatim from the 1794 edn.) of Toplady's *Works.*

35.   See *Works,* pp.610—663. Toplady followed this with *the Historic Proof of the Doctrinal Calvinism of the Church of England,* 1774.

36.   T. Wright, *op. cit.*, p.87. It is not really relevant to our purpose, but it is refreshing to pass from the heady atmosphere of the Calvinism/Arminianism debate to Toplady's casuistical excursus on 'Whether a highwayman or a cheating tradesman is the honester person'! (*Works,* pp.884—5). It is also strictly irrelevant to the *doctrines,* though illuminating as indicating the intensity of the debate, to observe the way in which the participants spoke of one another. Thus, Wesley wrote from York to Mr. Merryweather of Yarn on 24th June 1770: 'Mr. Augustus Toplady I know well; but I do not fight with chimney sweepers. He is too dirty a writer for me to meddle with; I should only foul my fingers . . . I leave him to Mr. Sellon. He cannot be in better hands.' (L. Tyerman, *The Life and Times of . . . Wesley* III,

p.83). To Toplady Wesley was 'the John Goodwin of the present age', whilst Sellon 'Stands in the same relation to Mr. John Wesley, that Caelestius did to Pelagius, and Bertius to Arminius; viz, of retainer-general and white-washer in ordinary . . .' (*Works*, pp.280 and 47). Among the epithets applied by Sellon to Toplady were: 'a flaming Calvinist, a Dagon, an Hooter, a Papist, a Socinian, a Mohometan, the greatest Bigot that ever existed, an Atheist.' (*Works* of Toplady, p.50). Sellon, opined Toplady, might have bettered himself — had he been born two hundred years sooner — for then, instead of being Wesley's 'pack-horse' he might 'as a reward for your meritorious denial of election, have been elected Tub Orator to the Pelagians of Feversham, or Booking'. (*Works*, p.60). This was not the worst that Toplady said of Sellon, but it will suffice.

37. The minutes are given in full by Tyerman, *The Life and Times of . . . Wesley*, III, pp.72—3; A. Stevens, *op. cit.*, p.203; A. W. Harrison, *op. cit.*, pp.205—6.

38. For Shirley see *D.N.B.* By an unfortunate slip Skeats and Miall place Fletcher in the wrong army when they give his work as *Check to Arminianism*: H. S. Skeats and C. S. Miall, *History of the Free Churches of England*, London: Alexander & Shepherd, n.d. but preface has 1891, p.374 n. See also *The Life and Times of Selina Countess of Huntingdon* by a member of the Houses of Shirley and Hastings, 2 vols, 1840.

39. Fletcher's second, third and fourth *Checks* were answered by Sir Richard Hill, his brother Rowland adding some remarks against the third *Check*. The fifth *Check* was a reply to Berridge's anti-Arminian work, *The Christian World Unmasked* (for Berridge (1716—93) see *D.N.B.* II, pp.393—4). Hill responded with *A Creed for Arminians and Perfectionists*. Fletcher's final response was *Fictitious and Genuine Creed*. For the course of the controversy see the relevant chapters in Tyerman, Stevens, etc. For a recent account of Fletcher's doctrine see D. R. Smith, 'John Fletcher, An Arminian Upholder of Holiness' in *The Manifold Grace of God*: London: Puritan and Reformed Studies Conference 1968, pp.61—75.

40. Quoted by G. Eayrs, *op. cit.*, pp.319—20.

41. A. W. Harrison, *The Evangelical Revival and Christian Reunion*, London: Epworth Press, 1942, pp.82—3.

42. L. Tyerman, *The Life and Times of . . . Wesley*, III, p.228.

43. Quoted by J. Orr, *The Progress of Dogma*, p.300, n.2. Though note the qualification of Professor Singer: 'The Wesleyan movement . . . in some ways bore a curious resemblance to the decrees of the Council of Trent in its denial of the eternal security of the believer.' C. G. Singer, *John Calvin: His Roots and Fruits*, Philadelphia: Presbyterian and Reformed, 1974, p.24.

44.   C. Hodge, *Systematic Theology*, (3 vols. 1871–3), II, pp.329–30.

45.   J. Wesley, *Works*, I, p.330. See Frank Baker, 'John Wesley, Literary Arbiter',*Proceedings of the Wesley Historical Society* XL, 1975, p.29.

46.   A Letter to John Newton of 14th May 1975, printed in Albert C. Outler,*John Wesley*, New York: O.U.P., 1964, p.78.

47.   *Whitefield's Journals*, p.587.

48.   W. Cunningham, *Historical Theology*, II, p.416.

49.   Susanna Wesley to John, 18th July 1725. See A. W. Harrison, *Arminianism*, pp.189–90.

50.   *Whitefield's Journals*, pp.573–4.

51.   A. M. Toplady, *Works*, pp.102–3.

52.   J. Wesley, *Works*, VIII, p.336.

53.   Dr. J. Ernest Rattenbury makes much of Charles Wesley's hymnological invective (and, incidentally, inadequately expounds 'Horribile') in his *The Evangelical Doctrines of Charles Wesley's Hymns*, London: Epworth Press, 1941, chapter VI. In the same chapter he emphasises, by contrast, Wesley's universalism: '*For all* Thou has in Christ prepared *Sufficient, sovereign, saving* grace . . .' (his italics). Earlier, W. Bardsley Brash had roundly declared, 'Calvinism had no song; it produced singers but they could not sing about Calvinism', *Methodism*, London: Methuen 2nd edn. 1930, p.101. But they could and they did! To take two examples which *emphasise* the gospel call:

    1.   'Come, ye sinners, poor and wretched,
            Weak and wounded, sick and sore,
        Jesus ready stands to save you,
            Full of pity, joined with power . . .' (Joseph Hart, 1759)
    2.   'Fly abroad, thou mighty Gospel:
            Win and conquer, never cease;
        May thy lasting, wide dominions
            Multiply and still increase;
        Sway Thy sceptre,
            Saviour all the world around'. (William Williams, 1772)

Lest it be suggested that we have overlooked those who might undermine our claim, we note that William Gadsby finds no difficulty in singing:

        'Love like Jesu's none can measure,
            Nor can its dimensions know;
        'Tis a boundless, endless river,
            And its waters freely flow:
        O ye thirsty,
            Come and taste its streams below.' (1814)

The majority of Calvinistic hymns (and we have not consulted modern, 'pruned' hymnals) appear to be in this vein on the question of the gospel call. Some Methodists may find this inconsistent, but they cannot deny that the hymns are there. Most Calvinists have ever maintained what the late Professor John Murray expressed so pointedly: 'If we fail to present this [i.e. the gospel] offer with freedom and spontaneity, with passion and urgency, then we are not only doing dishonour to Christ and his glory but we are also choking those who are the candidates of saving faith'. Quoted by Iain Murray, 'John Murray', *The Banner of Truth Magazine*, combined issues 143—4, 1975, p.56. In other words, the preacher must never cease to do what Christ did; and he came

> 'To make a proclamation free,
>   Of pardon, grace, and peace,
> The Lord Jehovah's jubilee
>   His year of sweet release.' (Ralph Erskine, 1732)

Further, on matters other than the gospel call, Calvinists can be quite technically Calvinist when they have a mind — as when Hart declares:

> 'Righteousness within thee rooted
>   May appear to take thy part;
> But let righteousness imputed
>   Be the breastplate of thy heart.' (1762)

Conversely, and against those of the opinion represented by Brash, A. H. Strong (*Systematic Theology*, p.368) says that 'even Arminians sing and pray like Calvinists' — and he quotes Charles Wesley to prove it:

> 'He wills that I should holy be
>   What can withstand his will?
> The counsel of his grace in me
>   He surely will fulfill.'

Doubtless the ambivalence just noted prompted the saying, 'pious Calvinists preach like Arminians, as pious Arminians pray like Calvinists': A. Mitchell Hunter, *The Teaching of Calvin*, Glasgow: Maclehose, 1920, p.129.

54. A. W. Harrison, *The Evangelical Revival and Christian Reunion*, p.79.

55. G. Whitefield, *Works*, London: 1771; quoted by A. Dallimore, *op. cit.*, I, p.406.

56. Quoted by A. Dallimore, *op.cit.*, pp.407—8.

57. *Whitefield's Journals*, p.575.

58. *Ibid.*, p.576.

59. *Ibid.*, p.578. A. Mitchell Hunter usefully contrasts Luther and

Calvin on this issue: 'Luther did not draw his assurance from this doctrine [i.e. the doctrine of predestination] and value it accordingly. He drew his confidence from the revelation of God through Jesus Christ . . . The doctrine was thus less to him than to Calvin and he often exhibited a "genial inconsequence" in his treatment of it. It could not but be otherwise with Calvin who found his unshakeable assurance in the certainty of his election mediated by the conscious possession of saving faith. This practical value of the doctrine he was never tired of impressing upon his hearers and readers, making it one of its chief recommendations.' *op. cit.*, p.98.

60.   *Ibid.*, p.583. Cf. Augustine, *On the Gift of Perseverance*, VIII 17.

61.   *Ibid.*, p.585.

62.   *Ibid.*, p.587.

63.   For instances of Wesley's opposition to antinomianism see L. Tyerman, *The Life and Times of . . . Wesley*, I, pp.481, 519, II, pp.400, 431; and Wesley's *A Blow at the Root* (1762), reprinted in A. C. Outler, *op. cit.*, pp.378—383. *Whitefield's Journals*, pp.323—4, provides an example of Whitefield's insistence upon works as a consequence of faith; and Toplady wrote a concise attack upon antinomianism, which concludes with the observation, 'That person must know little indeed of experimental religion, who can suppose that any pleasures or profits of sin, or all of them together, can compensate for one moment's loss of intercourse with God, as reconciled to us in his dear Son', (*Works*, p.432).

64.   A. C. Outler, *op. cit.*, p.31. Cf. the sermon of 'The Fulness of Faith', herein reprinted, pp.254—271. We should note that Wesley consistently maintained the doctrine of baptismal regeneration. See e.g. A. C. Outler, *op. cit.*, pp.124, 318, 321. The doctrine did not, however, loom unduly large in contemporary debates. See also R. N. Flew. *The idea of Perfection in Christian Theology*, London: O.U.P., 1934, chapter XIX.

65.   A. Stevens, *op. cit.*, p.215.

66.   Bogue and Bennett, *History of Dissenters*, I, pp.237—9.

67.   W. Cunningham, *Historical Theology*, II, pp.376—7; cf. p.510.

68.   Although we refer here to two parties, the borderlines between them were somewhat blurred, since methodists could be Anglican or nonconformist, Calvinist or Arminian. There were, moreover, some influential 'free-lance' ministers who neither engaged directly in the main debate of the day, nor paid much heed to denominational allegiance. Such a one was William Huntington (1745—1813), an independent who proclaimed High Calvinism — antinomianism, some said. He was honoured by many, especially by some Calvinistic Baptists — though he was a paedobaptist, and his own baptismal practice was spasmodic — and derided by some.

His principal anti-Arminian work is *The Arminian Skeleton* (1783). In the course of adverting to the difficulty of finding examples of *practising* antinomians Dr. Robison cites Huntington and the sodomist John Church as being among 'a few lurid examples of high Calvinist pastors of dubious character' (*The Particular Baptists of England,* p.72). Certainly Huntington was maligned by many, and his *D.N.B.* entry is by no means entirely flattering. T. Wright, however, attempts to achieve balance, and certainly reveals how difficult it is to establish the facticity or otherwise of Huntington's alleged *post-conversion* misdemeanours. Huntington not only admitted the sins of his youth, but employed them to illustrate the depths to which God's grace would stoop in order to redeem. See T. Wright, *The Life of William Huntington, S.S.,* London: Farncombe, 1909. Huntington's spiritual experience is recounted in his *The Kingdom of Heaven Taken by Prayer* (1784). He there explains his self-conferred 'degree' thus: 'As I cannot get a D.D. for the want of cash, neither can I get an M.A. for the want of learning; therefore I am compelled to fly for refuge to S.S., by which I mean *Sinner Saved* . . .' We should not forget either the evangelical Arminian thrust of the New Connection of General Baptists (1700), and their leader, Dan Taylor (1738—1816), for whom see *D.N.B.* and Baptist general histories.

69. See A. C. Outler, *op. cit.,* pp.427—472.

70. For Gill see *D.N.B.* VIII, p.1234; memoir concluding with Toplady's eulogy prefixed to J. Gill, *A Collection of Sermons and Tracts,* 2 vols., London 1773; The Memoir and eulogy also appear in the London 1830 edn. of Gill's *A Body of Doctrinal and Practical Divinity,* this being our source; John Rippon, *A Brief Memoir of the Life and Writings of the late Rev. John Gill, D.D.,* London, 1838; Walter Wilson, *op. cit.,* IV, pp.213—224; A. W. Light, *op. cit.* pp.123—30. Seymour J. Price, 'Dr. John Gill's Confession of 1729', *The Baptist Quarterly* IV, 1928—9, pp.366—371; B. R. White, 'John Gill in London, 1719—1729, A Biographical Fragment', *The Baptist Quarterly* XXII, 1967, pp.72—91. O. C. Robison, 'The Legacy of John Gill', *The Baptist Quarterly* XXIV, 1971, pp.111—125. There are two unpublished doctoral theses: Robert E. Seymour, *John Gill, Baptist Theologian (1697—1771),* University of Edinburgh, 1954; O. C. Robison, *The Particular Baptists of England* — the first chapter of which is the original of the article just noted.

71. In J. Rippon, *op. cit.,* pp.121—157.

72. A. M. Toplady in the memoir to Gill, *op. cit.,* p.xxii.

73. W. Wilson, *The History and Antiquities of Dissenting Churches* IV, p.221.

74. Quoted by A. C. Underwood, *A History of the English Baptists,* p.173.

75. See J. Fawcett Jr., *An Account of the Life, Ministry and Writings of the late Rev. John Fawcett*, 1818, p.94.

76. Quoted by A. C. Underwood, *op. cit.*, p.170. Hall and Evans are in *D.N.B.*

77. W. T. Whitley, *The Baptists of London*, London: Kingsgate, 1928, p.52. Mr. Kenneth Dix of the Strict Baptist Historical Society suggests that the figure of thirty may refer to the number of names on the membership roll, and not to the actual size of the congregation.

78. Horton Davies, *Worship and Theology in England, From Watts and Wesley to Maurice 1690–1850*, Princeton: Princeton U.P. and London: O.U.P., 1961, p.136.

79. See e.g. his *Biblical Predestination*, Nutley N.J.: Presbyterian and Reformed, 1966, chapter VI.

80. G. F. Nuttall, 'Northamptonshire and *The Modern Question*', p.115. Dr. Nuttall observes that whereas Hussey had been concerned with the *theological* point that to the elect alone is the gospel offered, the interest during the controversy over *The Modern Question* was *psycho-anthropological*. 'In this we may perhaps observe the effect, even within High Calvinism, of "the eighteenth century" ' (p.114).

81. See E. A. Payne, *Before the Start, Steps Towards the Founding of the L.M.S.*, London, 1945. One of the reasons for the secession of Erskines and their supporters in Scotland was that the Assembly would not accede to their request for the enforcement of evangelical preaching within the Church.

82. W. Wilson, *op. cit.*, p.222.

83. For Taylor see *D.N.B.* Cf. G. F. Nuttall, 'Northamptonshire and *The Modern Question*', pp.116–7.

84. For Daniel Whitby see *D.N.B.* XXI, pp.28–30.

85. But Dr. B. R. White has recently provided evidence which suggests that Gill was somewhat more of a man of clay than some of his supporters have believed. It appears that he may well, by doing nothing, have prompted the exodus of the supporters of his predecessor Benjamin Keach from his church. *Art. cit.*, p.85.

86. J. Rippon, *op. cit.*, p.56.

87. J. Gill, *Everlasting Love*, p.14.

88. For Hart see *D.N.B.* IX, p.62: Thomas Wright, *The Life of Joseph Hart*, London' Farncombe, 1910; A. W. Light, *op. cit.*, I, pp.203–9.

89. See S. J. Price, *art. cit.* The Confession is given in full in O. C. Robison, *art. cit.* and dissertation; and in R. E. Seymour's dissertation. The Confession was certainly modified in 1768, and

possibly modified in 1739. The amendments clarified certain points, but in no way toned down the High Calvinism of the statement. It has been suggested that perhaps because he thought Gill's Confession more rigid that Keach's, Spurgeon quoted the latter but not the former in his *The Metropolitan Tabernacle: Its History and Works,* London, 1876, p.36.

90. A. C. Outler, *op. cit.,* p.434.

91. *Ibid.*

92. W. Cunningham, *Historical Theology,* II, p.479; cf. pp.425—30.

93. See L. Tyerman, *The Life and Times of Wesley,* II, pp.191—3 for sufficient of this!

94. J. Rippon, *op. cit.,* pp.64—5.

95. Bogue and Bennett, *op. cit.,* IV, p.467. Not indeed that he was devoid of all humour: 'Dr. Gill, preaching a charity sermon . . . concluded thus: "Here are present, I doubt not, persons of divided sentiments . . . Those of you who are free-willers and merit-mongers, will give to this collection of course, for the sake of what you suppose you will get by it. Those . . . who expect salvation by grace alone, will contribute . . . out of love and gratitude to God. So between free-will and free grace I hope we shall have a good collection".' Toplady's *Works,* p.506.

96. See especially *A Body of Divinity,* pp.929—30.

97. E. F. Clipsham, 'Andrew Fuller and Fullerism', *The Baptist Quarterly* XX, 1963, p.102. He cites in support *The Cause of God and Truth,* 3rd edn., 1772, pp.49, 53, 72, 317, 339.

98. For Gadsby see *D.N.B.* VII, p.778; *The Works of the late William Gadsby,* London: Gadsby, 1851; and for a not entirely uncritical recent assessment of Gadsby by a Strict Baptist minister see R. Oliver, 'William Gadsby (1773—1844)', *Reformation Today* 8, 1971, pp.31—9.

99. See S. F. Paul, *Historical Sketch of the Gospel Standard Baptists,* London: Gospel Standard Publications, 1945. This variety of intro-spection is somewhat akin to that of those humble Scottish Free Church Presbyterians who were reluctant to receive the bread and wine at the Communion Service until they were sure that they had a saving interest in Christ. P. Toon has written a useful survey: 'English Strict Baptists', *The Baptist Quarterly* XXI, 1965, pp.30—36. In 1878, after heated discussion, the Gospel Standard Baptist Societies added four articles (nos. 32—35) to their Trust Deeds. The cumulative effect was to reinforce that clause in art. 26 which states, 'We reject the doctrine that men in a state of nature should be exhorted to believe in, or turn to God'. Gadsby's son, John, proprietor of *The Gospel Standard* was among the committee of nine appointed by the G.S. Societies

A.G.M. to consider the matter. See William Wileman, 'The *secret* history of the four "added" articles; 32, 33, 34, 35', *The Christian's Pathway* XXVI, Nov. 1921, pp.206–210; B. J. Honeysett, 'The ill-fated articles', *Reformation Today* No. 2, summer 1960, pp.23–30, reprinted under the title, *How to address unbelievers*, n.d.

100. W. T. Whitley, *Calvinism and Evangelism*, p.27.

101. Quoted *Ibid.*, pp.27–8.

102. For Fuller see *D.N.B.*; J. Ryland, *The Work of Faith, the Labour of Love, and the Patience of Hope Illustrated in the Life and Death of the Reverend Andrew Fuller*, 1816; G. Laws, *Andrew Fuller, Pastor, Theologian, Ropeholder*, London: Carey Press, 1942; G. Laws, 'Andrew Fuller, 1754–1815', *The Baptist Quarterly* II, 1924–5, pp.76–84; A. H. Kirkby, 'Andrew Fuller – Evangelical Calvinist', *The Baptist Quarterly* XV, 1954, pp.195–202; T. E. Watson, 'Andrew Fuller's Conflict with Hyper-Calvinism', in *How Shall They Hear?* London: Puritan and Reformed Studies Conference 1960, pp.22–9; A. H. Kirkby, *Andrew Fuller*, London: Independent Press, 1961; Ernest F. Clipsham, 'Andrew Fuller and Fullerism', *The Baptist Quarterly* XX, 1963, pp.99–114, 146–154, 214–225, 268–276; Jack Milner, 'Andrew Fuller', *Reformation Today* 17, 1974, pp.18–29. See also the unpublished doctoral dissertation by A. H. Kirkby, *The Theology of Andrew Fuller and its Relation to Calvinism*, University of Edinburgh, 1956; and Baptist general histories. Mr. Clipsham, in the second instalment of his work, justly takes Dr. Kirkby to task for seeing too direct a link between the writings of Calvin and Fuller.

103. In a letter preserved at Regent's Park College, Oxford.

104. For more on this theme see K. R. Manley, *John Rippon (1751–1836) and the Particular Baptists*, unpublished doctoral dissertation, University of Oxford, 1967. Garth A. Weston, *op. cit.*, is a mine of useful information.

105. For Jackson see W. T. Whitley, *Calvinism and Evangelism*, p.129; G. A. Weston; *op. cit.*, pp.4–5.

106. For Gifford see *D.N.B.* VIII, p.1179; A. W. Light, *op. cit.*, I, pp.69–71.

107. For an account of these appeals see K. Dix, 'Thy will be done : A Study in the life of Benjamin Beddome', *Bulletin* of the Strict Baptist Historical Society, No. 9, 1972. See also *D.N.B.* II, pp.97–8.

108. A. C. Underwood, *op. cit.*, p.142. John Ryland Jnr. seriously questioned this story concerning his father. See his *Life* of Fuller, p.175. Beddome served as settled pastor at Bourton from 1743–95, but he regularly supplied the pulpit there from 1740.

109. Quoted by W. T. Whitley, *Calvinism and Evangelism*, p.30.

110. Quoted by A. C. Underwood, *Op. cit.*, p.160.

111. W. T. Whitley, 'The Wallis House, 1792', *The Baptist Quarterly* I 1922—3, pp.160—1.

112. R. Hall, A. Booth and J. C. Ryland are in *D.N.B.* See also, G. W. Hughes, *Robert Hall;* London: Independent Press, 1961; E. A. Payne, 'Abraham Booth, 1734—1836', *The Baptist Quarterly* XXVI, 1975, pp.28—42.

113. For the text (2nd edn. 1801) see Fuller's *Works*, London, 1837, II, pp.1—125.

114. J. Ryland, *op. cit.*, p.141.

115. *Ibid.*, p.106.

116. For further details and sources see E. F. Clipsham, *art. cit.*, p.223. For Button see A. W. Light, *op. cit.*, I, pp.97—8.

117. J. Ryland, *op. cit.*, pp.566—7.

118. See *Institutes* III, xxiii, 13.

CHAPTER FOUR

1. *The Arminian Magazine* I, 1778, p.viii.

2. O. C. Robison, dissertation, p.153, citing J. Eyre, *Union and Friendly Intercourse Recommended.* There is a reference on p.154 to the essayist John Foster, to whom in 1809 Methodism was 'that odious and ill-defined mischief', but who, by 1814, was expecting incomparably more good than harm from Methodism.

3. For Williams see D.N.B. XXI, p.394; Joseph Gilbert, *Memoir*, 1825; W, T. Owen, *Edward Williams D.D.*, Cardiff: U. Wales Press, 1963, especially chapter VII; K. W. Wadsworth, *Yorkshire United Independent College*, London: Independent Press, 1954, pp.76—86.

4. W. T. Owen, *op. cit.*, p.95, quoting Williams's *Equity*, 2nd revised edn., 1813.

5. W. Gordon Robinson, *William Roby*, London: Independent Press, 1954, p.34. At the time in question Roby was working under the auspices of the Countess of Huntingdon.

6. *Ibid.*, p.43. Later still, during his Manchester ministry Roby wrote a *Defence of Calvinism* (1810) in reply to *St. Paul Against Calvin* by a Manchester clergyman, Edward Smyth. William Gadsby, then at the Baptist Chapel, St. George's Road, Manchester, also joined in the fray, as did James Turner. (So W. G. Robinson, *op. cit.*, p.168). Gadsby's pamphlet is entitled *An Everlasting Task for Arminians.* It appears in his *Works,* and has been reprinted by *Old Faith Contender*, Elon College, N.C.

7. Quoted by R. W. Dale, *History of English Congregationalism*, London: Hodder & Stoughton, 1907, p.705; also by A. Peel, *These Hundred Years*, London: Congregational Union of England and Wales, 1931, p.76.

8. Edward Morgan, *John Elias, Life, Letters and Essays*, (1844/7) London: The Banner of Truth Trust, 1973, pp.316—7, in a letter written on 24th December 1824.

9. For further details of the matters noted in this paragraph see W. T. Owen, *op. cit.;* D. Elwyn Edwards, *op. cit.*, Appendix. Elias, Evans and Roberts are in *D.N.B.;* R. L. Hugh, *The Theological Background of Nonconformist Social Influence in Wales, 1800—1850*, unpublished doctoral dissertation, University of London, 1951; T. M. Bassett, *The Welsh Baptists*, Swansea: Ilston House, 1977, pp.124—5.

10. Fergus Ferguson, *A History of the Evangelical Union*, Glasgow: 1876, pp.368, 370. The first draft of this statement was written by John Guthrie D.D. of Glasgow, p.371. For 'The Revolt [from Calvinism] within [Scottish] Congregationalism', see H. Escott, *A History of Scottish Congregationalism*, Glasgow: Congregational Union of Scotland, 1960, chapter X.

11. W. Cunningham, *Historical Theology* II, pp.507—8.

12. Quoted by Charles L. Warr, 'John Caird, 1820—98', in ed. R. S. Wright, *Fathers of the Kirk*, London: O.U.P., 1960, p.223.

13. J. MacLeod, *op. cit.*, pp.328—9. For John Kennedy (1819—1884) see *D.N.B.* A staunch defender of the traditional federal Calvinism, Kennedy's most sustained piece of theological writing is *Man's Relations to God Traced in the Light of 'The Present Truth,'* Edinburgh: Maclaren, 1869. In addition to those already mentioned, the following works bear upon the Scottish situation: H. F. Henderson, *op. cit.*, chapters VII, IX; John Tulloch, *Movements of Religious Thought in Scotland* (1885) Leicester University Press, 1971, Lecture IV; Harry Escott, *A History of Scottish Congregationalism*, Glasgow: The Congregational Union of Scotland, 1960, chapters X, XI; C. L. Warr, *Principal Caird*, Edinburgh: T. & T. Clark, 1926; Donald Campbell (ed.) *Memorials of John McLeod Campbell*, London: Macmillan, 1877; John Macquarrie, 'John McLeod Campbell', *The Expository Times* LXXIII, 1972, pp.263—8; J. B. Torrance, 'The Contribution of McLeod Campbell to Scottish Theology', *The Scottish Journal of Theology* XXVI, 1973, pp.295—311. Campbell, Erskine, Kennedy, Morison and Wardlaw are in *D.N.B.* John Caird is in *D.N.B.* XXI (Supplement). Campbell is also in ed. R. S. Wright, *op. cit.* Morison was influenced by the American Charles G. Finney.

14. J. Gadsby's memoir of William Gadsby in the latter's *Works* I, p.27n.

15.   For these see J. H. Philpot, *The Seceders*, 2 vols. London, 1931—2.
      For Warburton see his *Mercies of a Covenant God* (1837) Swengel
      Pa.: Reiner, 1971; for Kershaw see his autobiography, *John
      Kershaw* (1870), Sheffield: Gospel Tidings Publications, 1968.

16.   See his *A Concise Account of the Experience of James Wells*,
      London, 1840; R. W. Oliver, 'The Dangers of a Successful Ministry:
      The Life, Teaching and Influence of James Wells', *Bulletin* of the
      Strict Baptist Historical Society, 8, 1971. Mr. Oliver refers to Wells's
      controversy with Spurgeon in which the latter opposed Wells's
      anti-free-offer views; to Wells's part in the Eternal Sponship
      controversy of 1860—1, in which he maintained that Jesus was
      the Son of God *qua* mediator, but not by nature; and to the
      Rahab controversy of 1865, when Wells so interpreted the story
      of Rahab as to suggest that God of set purpose encourages
      duplicity in order to achieve his ends. Mr. Oliver does not mention
      Wells's controversy with Gadsby from 1844 onwards. This con-
      cerned Wells's view (which he renounced later, though never as
      vehemently as Gadsby would have liked) that 'a child of God
      cannot backslide'. See Gadsby's *Works* I, pp.85, 119—120 where,
      from the Gadsby side, evidence is provided to reveal Wells's
      'ungodly duplicity' respecting Messrs. Kershaw, Philpot, Warburton
      etc.

17.   W. Rushton, *A Defence of Particular Redemption* (1831), repub-
      lished 1973 by Primitive Publications, Elon College, N.C., pp.55—
      6. *The Gospel Standard* LXXXIII, 1842, p.318, welcomed
      Rushton's book as being an able attack on 'Fuller's sophistry and
      real Arminianism', and as a defence against 'that cobweb which
      Fuller's disciples are so craftily winding around the weak and
      wavering.'

18.   In a letter of 24th March 1842. See *The Seceders* II.

19.   G. F. Nuttall, 'Calvinism in Free Church History', p.426.

20.   For W. B. Pope see *D.N.B.* 1901—11, p.127; R. W. Moss, *The Rev.
      W. B. Pope, D.D., Theologian and Saint*, London: Kelly, 1909.
      H. B. Workman wrote of the 'triumph of Arminianism', one of
      whose marks was the repudiation of the Augustinian doctrine of
      total depravity. This repudiation made, the hypothesis of pre-
      venient grace saves the position from semi-pelagianism. To have
      shown this is Pope's 'most lasting contribution to Methodist
      theology'. *Op. cit.*, I, p.53.

21.   For C. H. Spurgeon see *D.N.B.* XVIII, pp.841—3. The English
      Strict Baptists, the Free Church (1843) and the Free Presbyterian
      Church (1893) of Scotland were among smaller bodies which
      resolutely carried Calvinism into twentieth-century Britain — the
      two last more ardently confessionally than the first. For these
      Scottish churches see (to mention only the most recent works)
      G. N. M. Collins, *The Heritage of our Fathers*, Edinburgh: The

Knox Press, 1974; ed. A. McPherson, *History of the Free Presbyterian Church of Scotland*, Publications Committee of the F.P.
Church, 1975. There being no complete Strict (as distinct from
Gospel Standard) Baptist history, it is not easy to assess the over-
all doctrinal position of that body. Many pastors were largely
self-taught, and comparatively few left a legacy of strictly theological works. But for an attempt to delineate the sturdy, independent Calvinism of one who wrote more than most see A. P. F.
Sell, *Alfred Dye, Minister of the Gospel* London: Fauconberg
Press, 1974.

22. See E. A. Payne, *The Baptist Union*, London: Carey Kingsgate,
     1959. Dr. R. T. Jones provides evidence of a decline of interest
     in doctrinal debate as early as 1858. In that year the *Evangelical
     Magazine* reviewer wrote of a systematic theology, 'If such books
     are read at all now, we fancy it must be chiefly by lay-preachers
     and bookworms'. In 1860 the *Eclectic Review* averred 'that
     people were tired of doctrinal extremes and refinements'. See
     Congregationalism in England, p.260. The activities and growth of
     such evangelical Arminian groups as the Primitive Methodists and
     the Bible Christians did something to foster the 'let's not split
     theological hairs' mood. For these see H. B. Kendall, *The Origin
     and History of the Primitive Methodist Church*, 2 vols. London:
     Dalton, c. 1900; John Petty, *The History of the Primitive Methodist
     Connexion*, London: Davies, 1864; J. T. Wilkinson, *Hugh Bourne*,
     London: Epworth, 1952 and *William Clowes*, London: Epworth,
     1951; Richard Pyke, *The Early Bible Christians*, London: Epworth,
     1941; Thomas Shaw, *The Bible Christians*, London: Epworth,
     1965. For one man's attempt to monitor the changing situations
     see R. W. Dale, *The Old Evangelicalism and the New*, London:
     Hodder, 1889. For accounts of some of the newer interests see
     A. P. F. Sell, 'The Rise and Reception of Modern Biblical Criticism:
     A Retrospect', *The Evangelical Quarterly* LII, 1980, pp.132–148;
     'Evolution, Theory and Theme', *Faith and Thought* CIV, 1977–8,
     pp.202–220; 'Conservatives, Liberals and the Gospel', *Faith and
     Thought* CV, 1978, pp.62–118.

23. G. F. Nuttall, in 'Northamptonshire and *The Modern Question*',
     p.117, citing Gill's *The Doctrines of God's everlasting love to his
     elect* (1732).

24. D. W. Simon, 'The Present Direction of Theological Thought in
     the Congregational Churches of Great Britain', *Proceedings*, Inter-
     national Congregational Council, 1891, pp.77–8. All this, be it
     noted in the very period which some of us were brought up to
     regard as the hey-day of preaching. Perhaps we need to dis-
     tinguish between oratory and proclamation.

25. R. W. Dale in *The Congregationalist*, 1877, p.5.

26. R. Mackintosh, 'Universalism' in ed. James Hastings. *A Dictionary*

of Christ and the Gospels, Edinburgh: T. & T. Clark, 1908, II, p.785.

27. We do not overlook the fact that in Britain since about 1960 there has been a revival of interest in Calvinism. Among the signs of this are the advent of The Banner of Truth Trust, and the formation and/or revival of reformed Baptist churches. These have ensured that the question of the free offer has been raised. See e.g. E. Hulse, *The Free Offer,* Worthing: H. E. Walter and Carey. Publications, 1973: and for opposition to what he describes as Fullerism, see R. G. Martin, *The Faith Once Delivered,* Epsom: Strict and Particular Baptist Ministers Fellowship, 1975. Again, in America David Engelsma is writing a series of articles in *The Standard Bearer* (commencing L, 13, Apr. 1, 1974) under the title ' "Hyper — Calvinism" and the Call of the Gospel'. See also John Murray and Ned B. Stonehouse on *The Free Offer of the Gospel* an undated pamphlet reprinted by the Orthodox Presbyterian Church (Philadelphia) from its 1948 *Minutes,* Appendix, pp.51— 63. See from the Arminian side ed. Clark H. Pinnock, *Grace Unlimited,* Minneapolis: Bethany Fellowship, 1975. But our point holds that such efforts are but peripheral to the main course of contemporary theology.

28. J. Zanchius, *Absolute Predestination,* Grand Rapids: Sovereign Grace Publishers, 1971, p.105.

29. Quoted by I. Murray, *The Banner of Truth Magazine,* combined issues 143—4, 1975, p.36. Cf. W. Cunningham, *Historical Theology* II, pp.510—11.

30. J. R. de Witt, 'The Arminian Conflict and the Synod of Dort' in *The Manifold Grace of God,* London: Puritan and Reformed Studies Conference 1968, p.19.

31. R. Mackintosh, *Essays Towards a New Theology,* Glasgow: Maclehose, 1889, p.424.

32. J. Duncan in ed. W. Knight, *Colloquia Peripatetica,* p.30.

Index of Persons

Printed in Great Britain
by Amazon